I will praise the LORD as long as I live;
I will sing praises to my God
all my life long.

Psalm 146:2

The Lord is my Shepherd; I shall not want.

PSALM 23:1

Advance Reviews for *Cancer Songs*

I found what I read to be comforting, to be rich in visuals, and easy to access, emotionally…. The religious aspect is present, but not overbearing. It provides a foundation, but doesn't shout over your story and overall message of hope.

Jennie Stockslager
Past Board Chair, The Noble Circle Project

When, in a support group for cancer survivors, a facilitator asked, "What keeps you going?" Judy Johnson responded, "I have a book to write." And a wonderful book it is. *Cancer Songs* collects reflections steeped in the psalmic tradition where poignancy emerges from thoroughgoing honesty, where joy gains depth and complexity through its encounters with unimaginable hardship, and where the isolation that so often accompanies personal suffering presents opportunities to till the soil in which restorative knowledge, sustaining communities, and resilient theology can take root. Like a treasured psalm, *Cancer Songs* offers the gift of sustaining words.

Deacon Rick Incorvati
The Episcopal Diocese of Chicago

Judy Johnson's *Cancer Songs* covers the gamut of emotions experienced by cancer patients, both during treatment and long after. This collection of meditations, written by someone intimately familiar with cancer, acknowledges these emotions and provides scripturally-based reassurance. This book is a must-read for anyone whose life has been touched by cancer.

Karen Herzog,
founder, Teal Loving Care, Cincinnati

With the elegance and specificity of a poet, Judy Johnson gives us a pathway through the psalms which are simultaneously modern and traditional. All of us touched by cancer will benefit from her Spirit-filled insights.

Gary Barker
Senior Associate Dean for Administration
and Undergraduate Affairs, St. Louis University

Cancer Songs

PSALMS FOR PILGRIMS ON THE CANCER JOURNEY

JUDY A. JOHNSON

ISBN 979-8-218-27223-4
edge street publications

Frontispiece: counted cross-stitch by Doris (Dodi) Holmes

Watercolors and poems by JAJ

Photo credit: Author photo taken by one of my nurses, May 2007, on my final day of chemotherapy.

Book design by Victoria Brzustowicz at Victoria B. Creative

Resources:

Metzger, Bruce Manning, ed. *The New Oxford Annotated Bible.* New York: Oxford University Press, 1991.

William Shakespeare. *King Lear,* Act V, Sc. iii
http://www.perseus.tufts.edu/hopper/
text?doc=Perseus%3Atext%3A1999.03.0029%3Aact%3D5%3Ascene%3D3

The Book of Common Prayer. New York: The Church Hymnal Corporation, 1979.

All Scripture quotations are from the New Revised Standard Version (NRSV) unless otherwise noted. Because the psalter in the *Book of Common Prayer* is arranged metrically, some of the verse numbers will differ from those in translations of the Bible.

This book is offered for the greater glory of God and in gratitude for all the medical people who have kept me alive to write it.

Contents

Prelude

In December 2006, following major surgery and a week in the hospital, I was diagnosed with Stage IIIB ovarian cancer, with a strong likelihood of recurrence. My recently acquired gynecologic oncologist wanted to use a new combo of intravenous and intraperitoneal (IV/IP) techniques. Despite having made up my mind never to go through what I saw a friend experience during her chemotherapy treatment, my own diagnosis made me so afraid of dying, I caved.

In January my gynecologic oncologist inserted a port into my abdomen for the intraperitoneal part of the treatment. I began chemo, managing four of the projected six rounds of Taxol and cisplatin. Then the doctors found a second cancer—bladder, Stage I, noninvasive—and then a third cancer, kidney, which cost me my left kidney and ureter. It was awful, but I'm alive, now seventeen years after my first symptoms.

I spent my early years among Baptists who believed that the Bible was to be read regularly and its wisdom and teachings applied personally. We were encouraged to memorize Scripture, even to find a life verse to guide us. After I became an Episcopalian, I settled on reading the psalms appointed for the day in the *Book of Common Prayer.*

The book you are reading is a compilation of some of the meditations I began writing during treatment. I wrote them for me, but also with an eye to publishing them later, so I wrote them for you, too.

Originally meant as a songbook for the Jewish people, the book of Psalms covers all human emotions. Cancer is an emotional rollercoaster—the sad, glad, mad, and scared, as one therapist put it. These selections are my response to the ancient words of the psalmists. Each of the five sections is arranged by the order in which they appear in the Bible. The meditations are deliberately brief, because we are all busy and may be in treatment, where we sometimes lack the focus needed for a lengthy read.

Judy
September 2023

Songs in a Minor Key

Songs of Fear

Scanxiety

Waiting for the giant white doughnut
to swallow me, a disembodied male voice
telling me
Hold your breath

IV in my right arm
arms positioned overhead
I stare at the ceiling's
four panels of painted pink cherry blossoms

against a blue sky unconcerned with warnings
about radioactivity posted everywhere in a room
where it is always spring.

Fridays

O LORD, in the morning you hear my voice:
in the morning I plead my case to you, and watch.

Psalm 5:3

I was supposed to be at the hospital for my chemo infusion two of every three Fridays during the four months of treatment. All the morning patients were due at nine. I quickly caught on that we patients outnumbered staff; one nurse was assigned to four of us. She dealt with us one at a time; she couldn't possibly insert the IV needles and start the lines simultaneously. I nominated myself to be her last patient, and was nonchalant about it when my drivers wondered why I was still eating breakfast at 8:30, even though we had a half-hour drive to the hospital.

"It's not like I'm going to a play or a concert," I said. "They can't start my chemo without me."

I am not a morning person. Year after year, however, I had been at work by eight or nine. Working as a freelancer, as I was during chemo, had allowed me to set my own schedule, to sleep in most days. Getting up early for a chemo treatment merely added insult to injury. But I had to get up. I had to take the very pricey new antinausea drug at a certain time.

One Friday I lingered over breakfast, then teared up as my driver sat patiently. "I don't want to go," I said.

"What's the worst part?" he asked.

How could I say? Where would I rank the sheer tedium of a fuzzy day in a recliner? Was the "big stick" when the needle pierced my flesh worse than the sledgehammer headaches and feeling bloated? Where would I place the need to go to the bathroom multiple times during my treatment day? What about

5

those siren-like sounds I heard most Friday evenings as I tried to sleep?

During most of Christianity's history, Friday was a holy day, set apart for fasting and prayer in remembrance of Christ's crucifixion on that day. It seemed altogether fitting that I spent not just regular Fridays but also Good Friday in the chemo room, hoping for my own resurrection.

After chemo ended, one dear friend and I exchanged e-mails for a while, marveling at the wonder of a Friday without chemo. Gradually, I stopped thinking, It's Friday and I'm not in chemo. I do remember that other people are there, and that Friday is my chemo nurse's day in the infusion room; I pray for them often, though not always.

Humans can't hold on to our experiences, whether they are mountaintop or valley, for very long. We make tabernacles, erect churches, light candles, compose music, write them down as best we can. Rituals help us remember. This rainy Friday morning, I am thinking again about where I was more than a decade ago, and how God has answered my prayers and pleading.

Torrents of Oblivion

The breakers of death rolled over me, and the torrents of oblivion made me afraid ...
[God] reached down from on high and grasped me;
[God] drew me out of great waters.

Psalm 18:4, 17 *Book of Common Prayer*

I have a friend who may be facing serious surgery. In discussing her options, none of which was attractive, she matter-of-factly said, "There's a real risk I'll die during surgery." Surgical risks are genuine, which is why the hospital staff scared me half to death before my major surgery, with warnings about what could happen and many pieces of paper to sign indicating that I would not hold the hospital responsible if any of them did. I remember wrinkling my nose as the education nurse explained the likelihood of waking up with a tube down my trachea to help me breath. I didn't want it and, as it turned out, didn't need it.

The *Book of Common Prayer* arranges the psalms for communal reading or chanting. It's the translation I read with breakfast, and it rivals the King James Version for sheer beauty of poetic language. (They were written about the same time, though both are updated periodically.)

This morning I observed that the narrator is passive in these verses. That is, he or she is not the subject, the one acting, but the one acted upon: breakers rolling over, torrents making afraid—and then God at work, reaching, grasping, drawing him or her out.

The verses make me think of the anesthetized, passive patient during surgery, with its risk of death, its oblivion, however temporary. I will think of this verse the next time I face an invasive procedure. Although the process does get easier—because I've had seven or eight surgeries in the last five years—they're never without risk, without a tremor of fear. I'm not in control—I'm not even conscious—but God is there, acting through surgeons and nurses and anesthesiologists, through the radiologist who reads the scans and the lab technicians who examine my cells. I am not alone, left to be roiled by the breakers or to drown in the great waters. The mighty hand of God is holding onto me.

The Gift of Presence

Even though I walk through the darkest valley,
I fear no evil; for you are with me;
your rod and your staff—they comfort me.

Psalm 23:4

Psalm 23 and I are old friends. More than any other Scripture, it was my comfort during chemotherapy. The beauty of holy words, however, is that new meanings can always be found. Just recently the basis for comfort became clearer to me.

The fact of God's presence is the foundation of fearlessness. Because God is with me at all times, even during surgery or in treatment, I do not need to fear. God is a companion—literally the one with whom I break bread—even on days when I can't keep down food. There is no place I can go to be outside the presence and persistent friendship of God.

Even though I'm in remission, I need these reminders. I'm about six weeks from my regular four-month checkup; I have already noticed the panic rising. When people ask how I am, I say, "I'm fine until they tell me otherwise." I feel fine, but I have learned that my sense of well-being is not finely tuned enough to detect the presence of cancer. I must wait for the test results. And I get a little crazy as they draw near, playing "what if?"—a game I cannot win.

Somehow, I never play a version of "what if?" that has happy outcomes. "What if I'm still clean?" never comes to mind. Instead, I imagine variations on "What if it's back?" I have a friend who prefers to surround herself with positive thinking and plays the game "Wouldn't it be great if … ?" She is clearly a better person than I am.

I am trying to learn to breathe deeply, to remember the reality that I am in God's hand, that I am not alone. I manage it sometimes. Before the last outpatient surgery, this spring, I remembered something that my priest had said in a sermon. I was able to walk into the cancer center thinking of her words, "God is already here before me. I am not alone." I know from my own experience that God is also in the chemo room, the examining rooms, the hospital ward. I know—through the companionship of my friends, both those with cancer and those who support me—that God does not leave us. I simply need to remember that fact more often.

Level Ground

My foot stands on level ground;
in the great congregation
I will bless the LORD.

Psalm 26:12

Mountains are awe-inspiring, but I don't much like them. I'm not fond of cities, either; I like to see where I am and where I'm going. I'm a prairie person; both mountains and skyscrapers get in the way.

Israel is hilly country, so I can only imagine the comfort that standing on level ground gave to the psalmist. Terra firma, we call it, ignoring the possibility of earthquakes.

This afternoon I returned to level ground after the funhouse-like effect of seeing on my calendar an upcoming checkup for ovarian cancer. I've spent the last few days feeling much as I did when trying to walk the first time I put on bifocals—the sidewalks kept coming up to meet me, the stairs were located in odd places. Perspective was skewed, if not lost.

Yesterday, for example, I couldn't find my driver's license. It was in my purse, right where it was supposed to be, but I couldn't see it. I was also having a mini-meltdown over my cat finding a second mouse in the kitchen. My stomach was upset. All because I was meeting my gynecologic oncologist, a man whom I dearly love—he did save my life, after all—who probably didn't have bad news for me.

Indeed, he did not. I am fine, he is pleased, and we will continue our twice-yearly meetings for another few years, after which I will come only once a year in perpetuity. I enjoy talking with him—he's one of those doctors who actually comes into the room, sits down, and doesn't take his eyes off the patient. We cover other, non-cancer-related topics; he sometimes asks about my writing.

I am, in so many ways, blessed beyond belief.

Lying About It

For behold, you look for truth deep within me,
and will make me understand wisdom secretly.

Psalm 51:7, *Book of Common Prayer*

I lied my way through church this morning. I figure when people ask, "How are you?" it's just passing social coins. Unless people already know what's going on, the expected answer is, "Fine, and you?" I rationalize that it might be different if I were—God forbid—on chemo and bald again, but few people at church know about the second cancer, much less that Friday will be my fifth surgery for it. The whole process of these recurring outpatient surgeries has begun to bore me, and—given my Little Red Hen nature—I didn't enjoy all the sympathy and help on offer when I did tell the truth.

That I attended church at all during chemo reflects no special virtue on my part. I'm wired for religion; I always have been. Being in a church where prayer has been offered for more than a century and every surface is soaked in words from the *Book of Common Prayer* gives me strength. Those words of liturgy and hymns offer great beauty. That's why I went on a morning when my body told me to stay home and listen to the rain on the roof. I went for purely selfish reasons—I wanted to sing (though I didn't feel like it), and I wanted the strength of the gathered community, however ignorant I've kept most of its members about my upcoming surgery.

I'm not sorry I went, just sorry that I felt fragile and distracted throughout the service. My urology surgeon has told me he doubts I'll need a temporary bag after this surgery, but it's hard to believe him, given that I've had one after each of the

13

previous ones. I was thinking about what I could wear to church next week that would hide the bag I may not have. One of the children has taken to wearing a bunch of plastic bracelets on his right arm, and I thought about bringing him my ovarian cancer one. And I thought about the plastic band a nurse will slip on my wrist in five days, and how much I hate that band, the sign of my membership in the company of the unwell. One dear woman touched me lightly on the back when she passed my pew going up for Eucharist, and her gesture nearly undid me.

The closing hymn included the words attributed to Francis of Assisi, "All you that pain and sorrow bear, praise God and cast on him your care." I lost it on that line—not, thankfully, with the immense sobs of which I am capable, but some tears trickled down my face. I wasn't in physical pain, but I was bearing sorrow, for myself and for friends undergoing various difficulties right now.

It's a humbling thing to have teenagers in my church who love me. I adore them and the fact that they come and sit with me after the service to tell me about their lives, just beginning to open, and to hug me.

The problem is that they're not stupid. One asked, "Are you all right?" Another came up, looked at my face, and wanted to know, "Why are you sad?" I gave them both the same half-truth, "Good music does this to me." Absolutely true, just not the whole truth. I was sorry I had to lie and that I'm not as good at it as I would like to be. As we waited in the line to shake the rector's hand, one of the young mothers in the church asked how I was. I told her I was fine, apparently believing in protecting the women and the children.

I left as soon as I could after that. There didn't seem to be any point in hanging around to enjoy fellowship at coffee hour and tell any more lies. We do what we can to get through these hard things.

Fearless Living

Whenever I am afraid, I will trust in you.

Psalm 56:3

We had a good soaking rain last night. This morning at breakfast, I noticed the drops caught in the delicate needles of the yew tree, shimmering in the sunlight like stars. The raindrops had nothing to do during their brief life except to shine. I knew that within an hour the sun would cause them to evaporate, but there they were, at that moment, reminding me of my mother carefully stringing lights on the Christmas tree.

The raindrops, so far as we know, are not conscious of their short life and do not fret over that life coming to an end. Both the Scriptures and great literature remind us as humans that our lives are also short. We are prone, however, to fret over this. And fretting dims our ability to shine.

There are so many things to be afraid of with a serious illness such as cancer. We fear the initial diagnosis, the surgery, the chemotherapy or radiation and their likely effects. We fear for our jobs if we are still working and the possibility of our insurance company denying a request for a prescription or test. We fear the effect of the illness on our family and friends. We fear dying in pain or drugged with morphine, leaving our true work unfinished.

But fear is a useless waste of energy, depleting whatever resources of time and energy we do have. Anger can provide fuel, but fear allows our strength to dribble out uselessly. It solves nothing, offers nothing.

The larger problem is that fear opposes faith. When I'm afraid, it's almost impossible to say the creeds with any integrity.

"I believe," I begin, and then wonder if that's true. How can I say I believe if I am living with fear? Fear will take over my life like a cockroach infestation, disappearing only if I turn on the light.

Meanwhile, I want to shine each day, be fully alive and present, instead of trying to live in the future, which I cannot know. I want to remember that I am caught in God's love like the raindrops in the yew branches, held for however long I am here.

No Fear

Whenever I am afraid, I will put my trust in you.
In God, whose word I praise,
in God I trust and will not be afraid,
for what can flesh do to me?

Psalm 56:3-4, Book of Common Prayer

If I think about it, there's a lot that my own flesh can do to me. It can make me miserable with chemotherapy reactions—sleeplessness, neuropathy, baldness, and itchiness, along with deep weariness that can't be erased with a good night's sleep. But I think the psalmist is speaking of what other people can do to me—the psalm's context is David's literal enemies, the Philistines, who are "hounding me all the day long," as the *Book of Common Prayer* expresses it.

Most of us spend a lot of time trying to please other people or wondering what other people think of us or our actions. This behavior was pounded into us early in life by well-meaning parents who told us not to pick our noses or let our slip or panties show. We carry it to school with us, wanting approval from teachers and peers. Many of us bear scars well into adulthood because we were always the last person picked for games on the playground. (I was a total loss at Red Rover; always afraid someone would hurt my hand trying to get through, I'd let go of the hand I was supposed to hold.)

Cancer can be a freeing of all that concern for the opinions and approval of others. Once you've lost all your hair, including your eyebrows, it's easier not to care what people think. When they see you in the grocery store, they may turn away from your drawn-on eyebrows or give you such a compassionate look that you want to cry. You have no control over these strangers' reactions, and slowly it dawns on you that you never did. An even greater comfort is realizing that, as a friend tried to tell me years ago, most people aren't thinking about me at all—they're thinking about themselves, as I am.

Not being afraid—that's a harder thing. The key is in the first line: trust in God, which is much easier said than done. One of the values of growing older, however, is having a history of seeing God at work and learning that God is trustworthy. This doesn't mean no enemies, whether human beings or wonky cells. It means that God is with us in every life event and intends good for us. We can trust and not be afraid.

In the Shadow of Your Wings

Be merciful to me, O God, be merciful,
for I have taken refuge in you;
in the shadow of your wings will I take refuge
until this time of trouble has gone by.

Psalm 57:1, *Book of Common Prayer*

*S*hadow has multiple meanings. We don't want one to show up on a CT scan. We may fear the shadow of death. We don't want cancer to follow us as a shadow.

And yet during chemo, when we are particularly photo-sensitive (as the fair-skinned among us are all the time), we seek the shadow of a tree. We're the ones always asking friends if we can move into the shade. Shadow isn't always a negative concept. According to this verse, we can take refuge in the shadow of God's wings.

I had a professor once who suggested that if we call Jesus the Lamb of God, we could also address him as Hen of My Heart. She was referring to the passage in the Gospels where Jesus anguishes over Jerusalem, saying he wanted to gather her inhabitants the way a hen shelters her brood under her wings (Matthew 23:37; Luke 13:34). Jesus wants us to be sheltered and safe, even during cancer.

September is Ovarian Cancer Awareness Month. You won't see the marketplace flooded with teal, or newspapers printed on teal paper. Ovarian cancer is deadlier than breast cancer, but it doesn't claim as many women. We don't have Susan G. Komen's foundation. Ovarian cancer is different than breast cancer—there's no screening test (though they're working on it), and there are no self-exams. It often hides among all the folds of a woman's body until Stage III or IV, when it is harder to defeat. The symptoms sound like any number of things, including aging: bloating, pelvic discomfort, digestive troubles, frequent urination. Detecting ovarian cancer, the Great Mimic, often requires multiple false starts—no, it's not a UTI, or a gall bladder issue, or menopause.

Yesterday was our annual walk to raise funds for ovarian cancer research; my only contribution for several years now has been merely to show up. In some ways, it's hard even to do that. We talk of those women we've loved and lost, who should still be among us; we monitor one another's progress, which is not always towards health. We move away from the afternoon sun to sit at picnic tables in the shelter house.

I asked a friend how she was. "Okay, I think," she said. "But you never know." She expressed what we all feel. Cancer is insidious; both of us could face recurrences at our next checkups, even though we felt and looked fine yesterday. During the progress of our disease, we will always need shelter under the wings of God—a shaded, dry place to rest.

Fear of the Enemy

Hear my voice, O God, when I complain;
protect my life from fear of the enemy.

Psalm 64:1, *Book of Common Prayer*

I can feel it beginning again, the cycle of fear that precedes my regular checkups. I get a little edgier, a little less patient with people (and patience was never my strong suit anyway). I can feel my heart rate go up; I need to take my blood pressure meds.

I don't like using battle imagery for cancer, but the psalms are filled with references to literal battles, so I revisit the metaphor as I daily read these ancient hymns. There's no way around the fact that cancer (if I choose to personify it) is the enemy seeking to destroy me—not only ultimately, but all along the way to ultimately. When I am in remission, the best way to destroy me is by fear. And there are so many things to fear: my own recurrence, the loss of health among my cancer sisters, the long-lasting financial repercussions of treatment. These debilitating fears all crowd around my soul.

Fear has no power for good. If cancer can make me afraid, then cancer wins, even if I never spend another day in treatment. The fear is a spikey fence, reminding me of the high walls I saw surrounding the homes of the wealthy in Santa Cruz, Bolivia during my mission trip there, working at an orphanage outside of town. The tops of those walls were fitted with broken bottles to deter any theft or invasion of privacy. Fear keeps my life small and fretful, all sharp, jagged edges.

So, it doesn't surprise me that the psalmist prays for deliverance not only from the enemy, but also from *fear* of the enemy. Cancer is a formidable foe, but it doesn't have the last

21

word. Elsewhere in Scripture, we are told that the last enemy that will be destroyed is death. Death's power is limited. I do not fear my own unbeing in the world I know, which will manage to go on without me. I'm more afraid of the prelude to dying: weakness, pain, loss of appetite. (How could life be worth living without being able to enjoy chocolate or fruit or cheese?)

If I spend my days in fear, though, I lose the joy of the present moment, which in any case is all that I have. I have only this day; I need to spend it more wisely than being afraid of not having another one, being miserly with my time and energy. Common wisdom for writers says spend everything you have on the page, each day, trusting that tomorrow the word-well will be replenished. It's good advice for life, too. I want to live each day in fearless wonder at its beauty. Fear is not a creative emotion, so I need to push it to the edges. I visualize fear as a literal bag of trash that I move from inside the house to the curb for trash pickup.

I have a friend who says fear is simply another name for the devil. When she reads any text with the words *devil* or *Satan*, she replaces that name with fear. Jesus confronted fear with the words of Scripture, with the command "Get behind me." We can patiently teach ourselves to respond the same way.

Refusing Comfort

I cry aloud to God; I will cry aloud, and he will hear me.
In the day of my trouble I sought the Lord;
my hands were stretched out by night and did not tire;
I refused to be comforted.

Psalm 77:1–2, *Book of Common Prayer*

Not to be offered comfort is one thing, but to refuse it is entirely another. By the end of this psalm, the writer manages to crawl out of despair. Still, the psalmist does so by referring only to long-ago history of the people, not to any present comfort.

I've read this verse many times over the years, but this morning it stopped me completely and sent me looking at other translations. None of them offer a cheerful variation.

Only once do I recall trying to refuse comfort: when my father died. I was living a thousand miles from my parents, in my third year of teaching, all of twenty-four years old. The call came during first period—the school secretary came to get me out of class. I went into shock mode, staying dry-eyed and making plans until third period, when my seniors demanded to know what was going on. One of them moved to hold me, and I protested, "Don't, Brian, I'll cry." But he held me and I did cry, aware that the girls in the class were crying with and for me. It's a holy memory for me, and the last obvious comfort I permitted. I had too much vested in my image. When I returned a week later, I was "fine."

Many of us have images to maintain. We're the parent, who has to stay strong or the kids will get scared. We're the spouse, trying to be strong for the beloved going through treatment. We're the son or daughter suddenly called on to be a parent to our parent in chemo. We're the person who's always had it together and can't let down, fearing we will never stop crying if we allow ourselves to begin.

And so, we're fine, even in the chemo room. I watched one day as a woman admitted to chest pains and was whisked into emergency so fast it made me dizzy. When her husband stopped in later, he told the nurse, "You don't see her at home, when she cries. It's really hard for her, but she tries to put up a brave front here."

Many of us did just that. We were ridiculously cheerful, making the chemo nurse laugh with our jokes and antics. I saw a woman who came in for treatment after work, wearing a stylish wig, nylons, and heels. I heard a woman facing recurrence say cheerfully, "Well, I've had three good years." I later joined their ranks. I lie at church and tell people I'm fine, two weeks away from another outpatient surgery for my "nuisance" cancer. Why bother them, when this has become my way of life?

This is my way of refusing comfort, even before it can be offered. I've been single all my life and taken care of myself; I don't like being dependent on others, although of course I am, daily. The problem, as someone finally pointed out to me, is that by always being fine, I'm depriving someone of a blessing. People *want* to help, and letting them do so is how we can offer them a blessing, by allowing their help.

Songs of Anger

Controlled Burn

We watched for weeks
as they prepared the old Barr place—
trees too near cut down
windows boarded up
roof shingles peeled off
safe perimeter marked with yellow tape
and then gasoline poured, match struck,
eager flames trying to escape out windows
only to be doused and contained.

It's like chemo, she said,
and I put my arm around her.
Yes, I know.
We, two sturdy brick fireplaces still standing,
watched the house come down.

When God Hides

Why, O LORD, do you stand far off?
Why do you hide yourself in times of trouble?

Psalm 10:1

Some days it feels as if God has found a great hiding place for a game of hide-and-seek. I cannot find God in my pain, or any useful purpose for being in pain. I cannot find God in any of the activities where I most often locate a sense of Someone paying attention and caring. Just when I feel I most need God, God appears to be absent. Or God is standing far off, watching from a distance, as if in the nosebleed section of a stadium, watching a game about which the deity has no strong feelings.

What good is that kind of God? I wonder, veering into anger. Because, of course, God exists to tend to *me* and *my* needs. Did we not have a deal? I would serve God faithfully, even working in Christian schools, and God would reward me—if not with a fat bank account, at least with good health. After all, when I completed treatment for scoliosis, hadn't I asked for no more physical problems? What had happened that suddenly my own cells were trying to kill me?

The issue may be with contemporary Western Christianity, much of which seems to believe that being a person a faith means no troubles will ever come. This idea is contrary to the life Jesus lived, to the experience of the early church under the Roman Empire, and to the wisdom of the medieval mystics.

Saint John of the Cross famously wrote about the dark night of the soul. Saint Teresa of Avila, writing to instruct the young nuns under her care, warned them not to be upset when God ceased to show God's favors, but instead to focus on helping

27

others. In one passage of her great theological work *Showings of Divine Love*, Julian of Norwich writes, "So I saw him [Christ] and sought him, and I had him and lacked him…" (p. 193).

When we feel forsaken—and we do sometimes have a right to feel that way—we need, as a pastor of mine once said, to back up until we get to what we know and are standing on solid ground. Perhaps in pre-cancer years, we felt secure in God's presence and love. We can remind ourselves of those times of faith and comfort, trusting that they will return.

Time Is Money

My times are in your hand;
deliver me from the hand
of my enemies and persecutors.

Psalm 31:15

"I don't have time for this!" is the cry of my heart. It's not just that I have surgery next week, but all the things that have to be done prior to that event. I've been told to get an EKG. I've managed to escape one for a few surgeries, but apparently have crossed some threshold. Tomorrow I will drive twenty miles each way to the nearest hospital-I-trust for the pre-surgery testing: EKG, blood work, and a urine sample, just in case I have a bad heart or an infection and don't know it.

"I'm fine! We don't need to do this!" I want to tell them all, but having a cancer growing in me for perhaps five years before it presented symptoms (which my gynecologic oncologist thought was the case for my ovarian cancer) shakes my confidence about what is going on with my body. I do know that the medical people have my best interests in mind—and that they also want to avoid lawsuits or the embarrassment of having me die on the table from some unsuspected heart condition.

It's the little things, always. Just this morning I've been on the phone to get pre-registered for my CT scan related to the first cancer, for the surgery for my second cancer, and for the EKG. Granted, a phone call takes less time than going in to the hospital or imaging center, but it breaks my concentration. As a freelance writer, I am nearly always trying to concentrate on something—this morning, I am way out of my league, trying to plan revisions for a piece on the International Space Station. Now, instead of getting back to work, I'm ranting on the page.

It will all work out. I "lose" tomorrow morning to an EKG, but my editors aren't calling for my arrest. I haven't been able to walk in the woods, one of my preferred methods of maintaining my balance; I've not felt that I had time, and it's been storming for days here. Walking would help.

"All shall be well," Julian of Norwich says. I expect them to find nothing on the EKG, and nothing on the CT scan, and nothing to indicate an infection that would mean rescheduling surgery. I need to stop complaining about the time and expense of all these tests and procedures and give thanks that modern medicine has kept me alive this long. I'll get right on that, as soon as I have time.

Using the Anger

Refrain from anger, and forsake wrath.
Do not fret—it leads only to evil.

Psalm 37:8

Survivors Teaching Students (STS) is a program of the National Ovarian Cancer Alliance. More than half the medical schools in the United States take part in the outreach to doctors-in-training. One goal of STS is to reach every medical school in North America. Another goal is to take its message to those in nursing schools, because nurses often can see the whole person and have time to share information.

Ideally, groups of four women—a facilitator and three presenters—speak of their experiences for an hour to medical students about to enter their gynecology rounds. Time for questions follows the presentation, which also reviews the symptoms of this deadliest of women's reproductive cancers and gives a human face to the disease.

When the nearby Wright State University's Boonshoft School of Medicine agreed to allow the program, I said, "Sign me up!" Along with half a dozen other women, I received training in telling my story: my symptoms, how I was diagnosed, what my treatment was, and where I am now. All this was to fit in eight minutes or less.

We've recently been invited to speak to two classes of future licensed practical nurses (LPN). It's been a different kind of experience. The medical school students have been receptive, but our message doesn't always seem to hit them personally. But the nurses-in-training, most of whom are women, have stories of their own to share.

One of the threads I notice among these women is anger. We who have cancer and those who love us are angry about many things, and justifiably so. The lack of a definitive test for ovarian cancer; the high cost of treatment and of insurance, which sometimes refuses to cover what we need; the unconscionable profits of the drug companies making the controlled poisons that have kept us alive; the petrochemical and agribusiness corporations that have poisoned our food supply and degraded the land; family members who perhaps put us at risk by their behavior when we were children; and the sometimes apparent indifference of medical people or family—it's a wonder that we don't self-combust from our anger.

We have a right to this righteous anger. The only problem is that anger alone doesn't help. If it motivates us to write letters and circulate petitions, well and good. If we use it as fuel to tell others what we've learned about things medical, that's terrific. But anger that simply smolders in us is corrosive and interferes with healing. We may need to journal our anger, giving it a voice; to do some serious weeding in the garden to expend it usefully; or to pray the imprecatory psalms, the ones that shock us with calls for vengeance. Yet the psalmist also encourages us to leave wrath alone.

Every person's anger will manifest differently, and recur to be dealt with again. Anger is a side effect that we can channel for good rather than letting it eat our joy or infect those we love.

In the Haunt of Jackals

Our heart has not turned back,
nor have our steps departed from your way,
yet you have broken us in the haunt of jackals,
and covered us with deep darkness.

Psalm 44:18–19

Some of us are quick to anger, a match struck and flaring briefly. Others do a long, slow burn, like campfire embers. Each of us has triggers; we may or may not know why certain things affect us as they do. For many of us, injustice is a key component in sparking our anger. "It's not fair!" children cry out, with the expectation of a just and proper treatment.

We can't know if the psalmist is angry, bewildered, or sad—or a blend of all three—in these verses, but I can understand being mad at God for perceived mistreatment. We did no wrong, the psalmist claims, our hearts and feet steadfast, but here we are, broken and in darkness, where the jackals—small dog- or coyote-like creatures—live.

Cancer might be considered a jackal, an omnivorous animal that sometimes hunts in packs. Each of us may have reasons why we were never going to get cancer—healthy lifestyle, no disease in the family, a person who helped others. Cancer didn't care.

"I'm too young for this disease!" I complained to one of my nurses. I didn't then know that girls as young as eight had experienced ovarian cancer.

"Anyone under 102 is too young for this cancer!" she replied.

Why me? is a fruitless question, with no answer. Good deeds and a righteous life are not protection. If we cannot blame ourselves (and we ought not), is it God's fault? The question is as old as Job. Like Job, we will not receive a clear cause-and-effect answer.

We may need to be angry for a while; it can give us energy to get through hard times. Ultimately, however, anger doesn't serve us. We are better off to accept our status as creatures, not gods, and to get on with the business of getting well.

Complaints

One of my friends complains that I complain; another, perhaps more like me in temperament, likens a well-turned complaint to a piece of performance art. I have told the quilters at church they have two options: I will complain if I don't have work, or I will complain if I do have work. There is, as I have often said, no pleasing me. Even so, I consider all this as simple kvetching; I am generally a happy person.

In the midst of all my complaining, however, I've realized an odd thing: I don't complain about cancer. It simply exists, the way dandelions exist. Some people fret about dandelions and try to exterminate them from a perfect lawn; others see great beauty in them. I know people who are grateful for their cancer and for its effects in their lives. I can't get there myself, though there are sub-categories for which I am grateful: skilled and kind medical professionals and advances in medicine that mean I don't have to die right now. But if I could pull out cancer by its roots and do something to make sure it never returned, I would.

I've noticed that I downplay cancer and its effects. This is not heroism but a dislike of being fussed over—except on occasion and only in the way I want it to be done. I don't complain about cancer, because doing so is a waste of energy. The cancer is utterly unaffected by my words—unless my gynecologic oncologist is right and survival can be predicted based on attitude. I do not intend to give cancer a greater foothold based on my gloominess.

Still, some days I am gloomy about nearly everything to do with my cancers, and some days I am simply angry. One of the beauties of God is that God is able to handle these emotions as easily as those related to joy or praise. God is interested in my total self, complaints and all, even if I come three times a day, as the psalmist wrote, and moan about my lot in life. God cares about honest communication and openness. God is big enough to handle the negative emotions that cancer and other difficult facts of life can produce. So, when I am ready to complain about cancer, it is God to whom I can always go.

Trials and Refreshment

For you, O God, have proved us;
you have tried us just as silver is tried.
You brought us into the snare;
you laid heavy burdens upon our backs.
You let enemies ride over our heads;
we went through fire and water;
but you brought us out into a place of refreshment.

Psalm 66:10–11, *Book of Common Prayer*

I disagree with the idea the God tests us or ensnares us, that God gives us cancer or allows us to have cancer (neither notion is satisfactory) as part of our personalized life curriculum. I've read the book of Job, and I have no interest in a God who accepts wagers pitting human loyalty against Satan's attacks. "As flies to wanton boys, so are we to th' gods; they kill us for their sport." Shakespeare put those words in the mouth of the Duke of Gloucester, in *King Lear.* A god who will kill us, or send us a disease that will kill us, or that will make us wish we were dead some days during treatment, is not one that I can worship.

I can find no purpose for cancer. Some people come to regard it as a friend, as the best thing that ever happened to them. Count me in with the people who think it's a calamity, for me and for them. Others say that cancer gave them the push they needed to become who they were supposed to be. I'd already been pushed and was fairly pleased with who I'd become in the second half of life. I know people who say cancer made them a better person. Cancer has only made me crankier and more impatient.

Perhaps I'm sick so that other people can watch me go through this. Maybe they can learn something in the process. This sort of thinking can allow me to slip into grandiosity quickly; observe sweet, lovable me, modeling how to survive cancer successfully. No doubt I have cancer so that my nurses and doctors could have the wonderful privilege of meeting me.

Nah, that doesn't work for me either.

My friend Maggie says that whatever is going on, it's bigger than we know. I no longer spend a lot of time trying to explain my cancers to myself; I try not to think with regret of the good old days before I became a statistic. I concentrate instead on the many places of refreshment that I do find in the midst of dealing with my cancers, on the friendships and opportunities it has brought me.

Weighty Matters

For my days pass away like smoke,
and my bones burn like a furnace.
My heart is stricken and withered like grass;
I am too wasted to eat my bread.
Because of my loud groaning my bones cling to my skin.

Psalm 102:3–5

These verses provide an accurate representation of what many people think of when they think of cancer patients—gaunt, wasted, sunken eyes. Even medical school students are prone to think that unexplained weight loss is a symptom of ovarian cancer. Just the opposite is true: it's the inexplicable gain that many of us experience, even when following a program of sensible weight loss, that's a tip-off.

A friend and I rejoiced in our weight loss post-surgery—each of us lost about twenty pounds once the tumor and various body parts were removed. "You've lost weight even in your hands!" a friend exclaimed after I returned home from the hospital. That loss was brief. My gynecologic oncologist warned me that most women gain ten to fifteen pounds on chemo.

I had intraperitoneal treatments—liters and liters of saline and chemotherapy drugs sloshing around in my abdomen on chemo Fridays. All of us in treatment knew to wear comfy pants with elastic waistbands to treatment. My chemo nurse told me that another patient had weighed herself before and after chemo; after her treatment, she had gained more than ten pounds.

It's true that some people get mouth sores because of their chemo and find it painful to eat. I did not. And much of the time what I wanted was comfort food that required little effort in the chewing department—mashed potatoes, mac and cheese, milkshakes.

The weight I'd lost after surgery came back. I have friends who have been unable to lose weight after treatment. I've not really tried. It's easy for me to slide into self-pity. *Poor me, with two cancers and now celiac disease, too! I think I'll have some more salt, fat, and sugar.* Knowing that this behavior is counterproductive (extra weight is not good for my knees and is a risk factor for a lot of other diseases) doesn't seem to stop me.

This sad reality is something I need to work on.

[Coda: A third cancer was later found, but I do not have full-blown celiac disease, only a sensitivity to gluten. I'm still eating salt, fat, and sugar.]

The Chemo Effect

I am deeply troubled;
preserve my life, O LORD, according to your word.

Psalm 119:107, *Book of Common Prayer*

"Chemo makes your eyeballs swell." It sounds like a schoolyard bully's taunt, but I heard it from my doctor; he was warning me not to change my eyeglasses prescription until I'd finished chemotherapy.

When I travel with a friend somewhere I've not been, I'm the person who gets travel guides and reads up on the place, suggesting interesting side trips. For the cancer journey, a chemotherapy information session—comparable to the education session that preceded my surgery—replaced those glossy travel guides.

First, though, the surgeon checked my port. He also took my right hand and placed it over the already-healing incision so that I could feel the port, a hard little knot below my right breast. I didn't like being able to touch it; the physicality of it made it difficult to dissociate from my body and intellectualize what was happening.

Doctors cannot tell their patients the truth about chemotherapy; the patients would run from the office as quickly as possible. They settle instead, as mine did, for "It's not your whole life, though it will seem that way," and "Your body won't look like your body for the next six months." But, no, dear doctor—a body exposed to toxic chemicals will never be the same again, even if the scars heal. Hair will grow back and mouth sores heal, but neuropathy and slight deafness may remain, and "chemo brain" is no joke.

A nurse shared information and risks about chemo from literature gathered in a two-pocket navy blue portfolio. I found the sheer amount of material overwhelming. According to the copy of the Chemotherapy Patient Education Form I had to sign at the conclusion of her presentation, the nurse covered the following side effects and concerns: "chemotherapy action, reduction in blood counts, nausea and vomiting, diet, hair loss, leakage from vein, numbness/tingling in hands and feet, allergic type reactions, sores in mouth, diarrhea/constipation, aching in muscles or joints, hearing loss, damage to kidney, bladder irritation, skin changes, and mental changes." They forgot the frogs and locusts. The brochure didn't mention bone damage, either, but I blame it for the osteoporosis and spondylosis that are now my spine's companions. By the time the nurse ended her presentation, I was nearly ready to give up and die of cancer before the combined horrors of chemo could finish me off.

I returned to my car with the friend who had accompanied me; I threw the navy portfolio into the backseat, where it stayed for nearly a month before I could bear to bring it into the house. Just listing the contents makes me angry at the damage my body took to stay alive, even though I'm grateful to *be* alive.

Songs of Sorrow

On Retreat

last night, storm
this morning, fog
both cleared off now
leaving only the drops
trees hungrily gathered

walking between summer-full maples
the stations of the cross
       alone as one must
my head sprinkled with the drops:
Godself performing the asperges
holy water from heaven
as trees rustle

The Sound of My Weeping

I grow weary because of my groaning;
every night I drench my bed
and flood my couch with tears.
My eyes are wasted with grief
and worn away because of all my enemies.
Depart from me, all evildoers,
for the LORD has heard the sound of my weeping.

Psalm 6:6–8, *Book of Common Prayer*

Years ago, when no one spoke the words "breast cancer" aloud, Betty Rollins wrote *First, You Cry*, one of the earliest published memoirs about the experience of having cancer. Tears are a reasonable reaction to what in many people's minds is a death sentence. Some people (like me) go numb and cry later, when the shock's novocaine has worn off. All along the way to renewed health (in one form or another), there are way stations for tears: painful or humiliating treatments, further bad news, or relief.

When my father died of a massive coronary, I was living and working a thousand miles away. I cried, went home to my family and cried some more, and decided that not crying was the better choice. In my almost-25-year-old mind, not crying provided a witness to how God could comfort us. I went back to my classroom and was "fine."

Except I wasn't. I cried in the shower in the morning when no one could hear me. And many nights, my roommate drove us to the ocean, where I sat on the seawall and cried, the sound of surf drowning my wailing. It took more than a decade for me to admit I needed therapy.

At some point, we're all cried out, at least for the moment. For me, the beauty of this passage in Psalms is that in the midst of the drenching and flooding, the wasting and wearing away, we know that God hears us. In another psalm, the writer asks that God put the tears he's cried into a bottle. I don't know how that would help, but perhaps it's meant as a sign that the tears have value, the way that items in a museum exhibit have value. Ah, these are the tears she wept for her father. These are her cancer tears. See the differences, note the beauty of both.

There's no shame in weeping. We need the tears as an emotional release. They soften us, breaking down the illusion of separateness and independence we sometimes try to maintain. We have a right to our tears, and no one can tell us when it's time to dry our eyes. We will know.

Heart Trouble

Turn to me and be gracious to me,
for I am lonely and afflicted.
Relieve the troubles of my heart,
and bring me out of my distress.

Psalm 25:16–17

As if cancer and its treatment aren't bad enough, many of us also have to contend with what the psalmist terms "troubles of the heart." Sometimes these take a physical form—one day, one of the women in the infusion room complained of chest pains, sparking a medical emergency response that was impressively prompt. (Her heart was fine, we learned later. Stress can do that to a heart.)

Most of the time, though, the heart trouble isn't literal. We fret over so many things—the dread of leaving our families and friends, of not completing our contribution to the world, of painful dying. And there's existential sadness in the knowledge that after a time of mourning, the people in our world will go on without us. Life doesn't stop when someone we love dies. We know this from experience, but find it hard to accept when considering our own dying.

We may scare ourselves with dark imaginings that can cause our hearts to beat faster. Although it's natural to be afraid when we face surgery or treatment, we need not exaggerate the fear. I can be a drama queen myself, but it wears on others, who have their own heart issues.

The psalmist asked God to relieve the distress, and that's a fine prayer. But we can also take steps to alleviate our distress. For one thing, we can stop thinking fearfully. Replace fear with cheer.

I don't mean to sound Pollyannaish, but there's something to all this positive thinking, and being afraid isn't a strong position.

At the beginning of our collaboration, my gynecologic oncologist told me that attitude was the best predictor of success in cancer treatment. I have seen this fact played out in women who have lived well and fully in the midst of treatment and recurrences. As one friend puts it, choosing joy is key. Taking time to notice and delight in each day's gifts is also crucial. God's mercies are new and fresh very day, the book of Lamentations tells us.

Now, many years after the end of my chemo regimen, I've seen women get very sick and leave this life unexpectedly and quickly. I know that there are no guarantees. My hope is to find some joy each day, so that I am fully present to whatever blessings arrive, rejoicing in whatever God sends to relieve my heart troubles.

Outsider

My friends and companions
stand aloof from my affliction,
and my neighbors stand far off.

Psalm 38:11

We can only be grateful that attitudes about cancer have changed. It is no longer a disease that people whisper about or shelter children from knowing about, as if it were shameful. In the past, sometimes doctors didn't even tell their patients they had cancer. Much attention is now focused on cancer walks and other fundraisers, celebrities with cancer, cancer ribbons. Support groups abound. Cancer is no longer an automatic death sentence, and for that we can rejoice.

And yet. Some people still avoid a cancer person, don't make eye contact in the grocery store, as if cancer were contagious. A bald woman—even in a wig, a scarf, or a hat—can still be considered a frightening sight. We might be able to cover our heads when bald, but the drawn-on eyebrows and the lack of lashes are a giveaway.

A woman in my support group told us recently that she went up to a woman in a store, seeing that she was obviously in treatment. She wanted to encourage her with her own recovery, spread the word about our group. I applaud her for that; it's not something an introvert like me would readily do. I'm more likely to come out of my private fog, realize *That's a wig*, and then pray silently for the woman. I hope both approaches are valuable.

I'd resisted joining a cancer support group. Having watched a dear friend go through chemo, I thought I knew what I could expect. What no one explained to me, however, was the mental, emotional, and spiritual isolation that cancer may bring. I'm sure not everyone experiences this state of feeling different because of cancer, but I found it a relief to be with my "cancer sisters." They knew what a chemo room looked like, had been through surgeries as well, had come to love their doctors for both their skill and their empathetic wisdom. There was no need to "protect" anyone else by being less than honest about what I was experiencing, though I was still trying to be "the best little cancer patient ever," as I told my own doctor. (He turned to the nurse in the room and said, "We should put that on pillows and give them out." She pragmatically suggested that if everyone had one, it would dilute the sentiment.)

One of the catch phrases of my youth was "Get real." I found that goal a challenge with cancer, thinking most people aren't ready to hear about the reality of cancer. Being with my "cancer sisters" removed the need to hide. The support group I didn't want to join became one of the salvific things about cancer.

Liquid Heart

My soul melts away for sorrow;
strengthen me according to your word.

Psalm 119:28

Trust in him at all times, O people;
pour out your heart before him;
God is a refuge for us.

Psalm 62:8

We use heart to stand for all our feelings, for our emotional state. "My heart melts," a friend of mine says about his response to babies, a class of people of whom he's very fond. "I melted," we sometimes say about the effect of a look or word from the beloved. But melting also occurs in sorrow, as the psalmist knew. Sometimes the heart feels heavy with sorrow; at other times, it feels liquid.

One of the good things about liquids is that they pour more easily than do solids. We melt butter in a pan over flames; our hearts are melted in the fires of adversity. Sometimes that fire isn't a metaphor—"liquid fire" is what my chemotherapy nurse called the shot of Aranesp I received to keep up my white blood cell count during treatment. I could feel it burning as it traveled up my arm, the large molecules straining to move through the veins.

The Bible is full of warnings against having a hard heart. I don't know any more effective means than an incurable disease to soften and liquify the heart. In treatment, I watched the women going through chemo a second or third time; they seemed incredibly cheerful to me. I didn't see one woman who was resentful or angry about being back in treatment. They had each achieved a liquid heart.

In chemo, I could feel my heart becoming a sopping liquid mess, and I was too tired from treatment and fear to pull myself back into a solid state. When all the needles were removed, I oozed from my recliner to my designated driver's car. Riding home, I looked out the window at the bright day or the falling snow. And I poured out my liquid heart to God about it: *I don't like this. Please don't ask me to do this again. I don't think I can go through it again.* I'm sure it's the same prayer every person with cancer prays. And sometimes there seems to be no response, or the response feels like a shrug and an insincere, "Sorry."

Somehow, we find the courage (a word rooted in the French word for heart) that we need to face our days and our sorrows. God is our refuge. We do not need to steel ourselves, harden our hearts again. Instead, we keep before us both the possibility of a recurrence and the hope of resurrection. And we pour out our liquid hearts to God.

Left Alone in the Dark

My friend and my neighbor you have put away from
me,
and darkness is my only companion.

Psalm 88:18, *Book of Common Prayer*

To be honest, I have never felt the degree of isolation this psalmist describes. I *have* experienced a horrible inversion of it, days when I wish my dear friends and neighbors would go away and leave me to the darkness. But not for very long, only for a little while, and only on a day when I wanted to be left alone. Other days, I yearn for human contact, some distraction to divert my thoughts onto a different path.

Today was one of the days when I could barely stand other people and wasn't fond of my own company either. I do not know what prompts such days; I only know that by the time I was eating breakfast and reading Psalms, I was praying my most desperate prayer: *Please don't let me hurt anybody.* Because I knew that today I was capable of wounding, carelessly and with glee.

Many years ago I heard a performance of a piece written by Tim O'Brien, a Vietnam veteran, recalling a man who adopted a puppy while he was serving overseas. Each night he would twist the dog's paw until the poor creature cried. He explained that he did so because he wanted something else to hurt as much as he did. (Thankfully, his actions didn't square with the person he thought and wished himself to be; he gave away the dog.)

When I listened to that piece being performed, I was horrified, but now I understand a bit of that serviceman's feelings. I occasionally want to lash out at someone else, too, to make them feel as hurt and bewildered as cancer has left me.

Where did *that* come from? What did I do to deserve *that?*

Nothing. You did nothing, and neither did I. These miserable days are hard to explain, even to myself—emotional ambushes, like snipers on the Ho Chi Minh Trail. There is just this darkness that comes.

I remember that when a friend was undergoing treatment for cancer several years before I was diagnosed, I just wanted her to *eat.* I'd make pretty food that seemed easy to get down, easy to digest; if she ate any of it, I'd leave with a sense of pride. When I was in treatment, I finally understood why she didn't care about eating. I apologized to her for being so "helpful."

Does this mean we shouldn't take food to people on chemo, or invite them to outings, or call them to check in? No. Everyone responds differently to treatment and to kindness. Most days, I am more than glad to hear from friends and neighbors.

On dark days, which don't come often, I pray that people will stay away. I try all my usual remedies: music, chocolate, the cats, a walk in the woods, a cup of tea, a nap, and writing. I pray not to hurt anyone. I wait for the miserable mood to go away, listening for the sound of a rescue plane.

Our Frail Flesh

Remember, LORD, how short life is,
how frail you have made all flesh.
Who can live and not see death?
who can save himself from the power of the grave?

Psalm 89:47–48, *Book of Common Prayer*

Another of my ovarian cancer sisters died recently. It doesn't matter that we had been together only a handful of times since I'd first met her. By then, she was already declining, but bubbly still, with flashes of wit and insight that let me know this was no dotty woman a few years my senior. The care and devotion her sister gave was enough to make me once more regret never having had a sister.

I watch those of us with cancer trying treatments that promise to extend our lives. Some opt for clinical trials, like the woman at my church who told me that the treatments hurt, but she would do anything to keep one more person from having her rare cancer. Others try a different chemotherapy drug when the cancer comes back, or head for more surgery.

We are all going to die. We forget this in the midst of busy lives and just-around-the-corner dreams and goals. I once regularly told God on my walks in the woods, "I want to walk these paths for another twenty years, please." I imagined myself, possibly frail enough to need a walking stick even when walking on level ground, or in a motorized wheelchair hitting trails that accommodated such vehicles. After my first surgery, what I most wanted was to get back to the woods; I was grateful to the friend who took me there and made sure I didn't overdo it that frosty morning.

Now the idea of another twenty years seems preposterous some days. According to statistics that my oncologist urges me to ignore, I have a 50-50 chance of surviving for five years with ovarian cancer. (He says the stats are not accurate, lumping all patients together, when some of us have improved our odds through a successful surgery or enough chemo). I feel fine today, but I've learned that how I feel doesn't mean anything.

Our flesh is frail. I didn't know this in my early and midlife years. Not really, not in my body. I was never athletic or especially graceful, and I've spent many years living in my head only. But I could count on my flesh to be there—it was sturdy and complained very little. Now, between the cancer that revisits and the normal aging processes, I am aware of my frailty.

We are all going to die. The good news for most of us is, not today. How, then, to invest these twenty-four hours with meaning and goodness? I will assume I am going to continue to be, for today at least, and I will not let myself be consumed by the trivia and effluvia of the wider culture. Do what matters, hopefully for someone besides myself. Because my flesh is frail, too, and I will not be here forever.

[Coda: Currently, I've survived seventeen years beyond the first surgery. I've dealt with multiple cancers, but the ovarian cancer has never recurred.]

Brought Very Low

*The L*ORD *watches over the innocent;*
*I was brought very low, and [the L*ORD*] helped me.*
Turn again to your rest, O my soul,
*for the L*ORD *has treated you well.*
For you have rescued my life from death,
my eyes from tears, and my feet from stumbling.

Psalm 116:5–7, *Book of Common Prayer*

In one sense, all cancer patients are innocent before the first chemo or radiation treatment, which is an initiation ceremony like no other. I did well in chemotherapy, as my nurse kept telling me, despite how awful I felt in mind and body. Often during those four months, however, I found myself thinking, *I had no idea.*

Cancer seems to me one of the most potent ways to be brought very low. Along with the reality that our lives are at risk, the indignities of treatment also bring us low. Most women I know regard losing their hair as a loss that cannot be made right with the simple assurance, "Hair grows back," or the brusque encouragement, "Be glad you're alive." In addition, once we realize that we are going to live (for now, this time), we must deal with insurance forms and ever-mounting bills resulting from our attempts to monitor the disease and to remain well.

Eventually we regain the strength we'd lost to the powerful drugs. "You won't feel like yourself all at once," my oncologist told me when releasing me for three months after chemotherapy ended. Friends who had firsthand experience with chemo said I'd need a month to six weeks before I would feel something like myself.

Although I had days near the end of my chemo treatments when I took three naps, I was determined to regain strength and stamina. I began walking half a block, then a full block, then two. At first the walks were a chore, and I carried a treasured walking stick because I felt unsteady; soon it felt good to move freely again.

Hair does grow back, slowly, although perhaps not the way it used to look. Mine was curlier than usual. Friends thought it was darling; I hated it, even though I was glad not to be bald. Every time I looked in the mirror, I was reminded that I'd been in chemo, and that it continued to affect me. Because I was trying to avoid anything that might set off mutant cells, I quit coloring my hair, which was a gray-brown mix. The first time I needed a haircut, I looked at the wisps lying feathery on the black cape and told my stylist, "It looks like rabbit fur," and he had to agree. He said it would take perhaps eighteen months for my hair to regain its usual texture, and he was right.

We do turn again to a more restful soul, as the psalmist said, although we may find a new vigilance in that soul. We feel and express our gratitude to God, to our treatment team, to our family and friends who have sustained us. We stop crying, walk without stumbling, and have the beautiful sense that we *have* been rescued.

Still Singing

How shall we sing the LORD's song
upon an alien soil?

Psalm 137:4, *Book of Common Prayer*

Had we been living in Israel in 586 BCE, we would likely have been among those captured when the nation came under the power of Babylon. Resettlement and eventual assimilation comprised that empire's foreign policy. As faithful Jews, we might have wondered what God was doing; we may have resisted the tendency to settle down with foreign spouses and make the best of it.

Perhaps on the way to Babylon, or soon after we arrived and were still marked as outsiders, someone said, "Sing us a song of Zion." They might have been mocking, or they might have been genuinely interested. We would stand mute before them—how could we sing the LORD's song upon an alien soil? Singing the LORD's song in Babylon might have even seemed blasphemous.

When we first enter Cancerland, we stand on alien soil. We are held in thrall to many varieties of medical people, who are ranked as plainly as in any military. They all speak—and may not define clearly—in a new, unwelcome tongue. New customs, such as a chemotherapy regimen or radiology sessions, become part of our daily lives. Most of us resist assimilation. We are here against our wills and don't want to get too comfortable here. We pray for this to be just a detour, not a new highway on which we will travel for the rest of our lives.

Singing the LORD's song sometimes feels impossible. How can we praise God, rather than cast blame? Or sing, when all we want to do is weep or rage? And yet, God wants our voice, albeit ragged with tears, as part of the daily chorus of praise. There is always something for which we can be thankful: a skilled nurse who inserts the IV needle painlessly and in the right vein the first time; another patient who makes us laugh; the cool glory of cheesecake, perhaps one of the only foods we can keep down.

Singing isn't just for God, or for the benefit of those around us who need to know we are okay. Singing is good for us, a positive force for healing. When I was in chemo, I wasn't sure if I could commit to the demanding rehearsal schedule and performance of Beethoven's *Ninth Symphony* with the Springfield Symphony Chorale. The conductor kindly suggested that I come to rehearsals for as long as I could, whether or not I could perform. "Music is so healing," he said. I found that singing this affirmation of joy with eighty other people filled me with hope, even as I grew weaker and wearier from treatment.

Ultimately, I wasn't strong enough to perform in May. The concert coincided with my final treatments, and I didn't think I could stand long enough to sing, even if I had enough breath to hit the notes. The whole experience, however, taught me something about singing the Lord's song on alien soil—we must do it.

[Coda: Several years later, the orchestra and chorus again performed the Beethoven *Ninth Symphony*—and I sang with them.]

Fainting, Failing Spirit

My spirit faints within me;
my heart within me is desolate.
O LORD, make haste to answer me;
my spirit fails me.

Psalm 143:4, 7, *Book of Common Prayer*

Within three short verses the psalmist's spirit spirals down from fainting to failing. In between, the writer muses on all God's deeds and considers the work of God's hands. I'd think that would help to prevent such a drop, but no.

The truth is that some days nothing helps. Walking the cancer journey is like traipsing through a bog—the ground looks solid, and then I sink. Although I don't like them, these mood dips don't surprise me anymore. They're just part of the package. Few people can sustain cheerfulness indefinitely, and it's hard to be cheery when slogging through the trough of chemo or a recurrence.

The temptation is to wallow, and I am a champion wallower. Just now, it's gray and raining outside. As a result, every day new leaves appear on the trees around my home. Despite that fact, I fight the urge to go back to bed and stay there for a few weeks, until I recover from this upcoming surgery I don't want.

My spirit is fainting because I've had expectations that haven't been met. The cancer wasn't supposed to come back. I wasn't ever going to need the services of the prestigious cancer center an hour north. It's the place I've always considered the court of last resort, even though my gynecologic oncologist truly and sensibly tells me it's where I'd go first if I lived in that city.

My spirit faints because I am again facing the dilemmas of who to tell, when and how to tell them, how much to say, and what to answer when they ask how they can help. Most people do ask; I have no answer. A new immune system? Thousands of dollars to cover my growing medical expenses? How about courage, or even faith that there will be a happy ending? Can you be here at four in the morning when I wake up afraid?

What I'm learning is that—regardless of cancer—I have to show up for my life. Going back to bed is a luxury denied me. I have work to do and a friend who is coming to cheer my fainting spirit. We are going to an art show and to a farmer's market, and if that doesn't help my spirit, I will be surprised. I must keep working through it, riding the emotion and not worrying too much about it. God has many other ways to revive my spirit; I will keep looking for them and waiting.

After

Let me hear of your loving-kindness in the morning,
for I put my trust in you;
show me the road that I must walk,
for I lift up my soul to you.

Psalm 143:8, *Book of Common Prayer*

I needed this verse more after chemo ended than I had during the Fridays of Taxol and cisplatin. During those months of treatment, I knew where I had to walk—straight to my navy blue recliner in the chemo room. For two of every three Fridays I was in chemo for much of the day. The first week involved a double whammy: IV/IP, which meant that I received drugs both intravenously and through a port intraperitoneally (into my abdomen). The process took most of the day, nine to five, as if I were one of those people still going to the office. The next week was a shorter day, with only IV therapy. The treatment usually was finished by early afternoon on those days. I had one week to begin to feel better, and then we repeated the cycle, for four months.

For me, finishing chemo was a case of "Goodbye treatment, hello post-traumatic stress." Treatment wasn't any fun; however, it did require a lot of energy and determination, and it bought me and my new friends from the chemo room a lot of attention. Now we were whole, or reconstructed, and everyone had disappeared. Our regimen had changed, too; the calendar wasn't filled with chemo or radiation appointments or blood draw reminders.

On top of that, we'd lost the camaraderie of our nurses and our new chemo buddies. We had finally found a place to be completely real, where we could discuss anything deemed not polite conversation: baldness, constipation, mouth sores— nothing was too private. Suddenly, happily, we were told we're in remission and free of the hospital for three months.

I had a difficult time with that freedom, frankly. In some ways it was harder than adjusting to having cancer, to treatment. I had all this free time—Fridays were no longer built around trips to the hospital. I slowly began to regain strength and hair.

Once I wasn't actively in treatment, who was I? I certainly couldn't go back to the old ways of thinking, as some people manage to do. Cancer wasn't merely having the rug pulled out from under me—someone had taken the rug and disposed of it! I always knew I would have to die someday; I'd gotten a reprieve, but I was, like everyone else, mortal. In a different way than I'd known before diagnosis, I knew I would die.

The high drama of surgery and treatment ended; nothing as major was then at stake. To create writing that reaches others, we're told, something big has to be at stake. Surviving treatment was big. Figuring out how to live once that treatment ended wasn't.

Ending treatment was an odd kind of grief. I'm on my own again now—not entirely, but to a greater degree than I was during treatment. Flowers, calls, cards, minestrone soup went to others in active need. Some days I struggled with survivor's guilt—at this writing, I've not experienced a recurrence of my dangerous cancer. I met women in the chemo room a few years years ago with my same cancer who are no longer alive. I missed their wit and courage, even though I knew them only in one context, briefly.

In many ways, I was still me. Still writing, still walking in the woods along the river, still loving good food and conversation. In other ways, I felt both loss and lost. I needed to know how to walk this Survivors' Road. For that, for everything, I must look to God.

Songs in a Major Key

Songs of Joy

Survivor

Tonight's perfection—
walking along the river,
purple flowers bordering the path,
geese calling, flying above the river,
slowly driving out of the park,
sunroof open, one hand conducting
the last movement of Mozart's final symphony,
to the left a young deer, listening, startled,
showing me his white tail.

I think of Mozart, dying young,
myself greedy for life, glad for this year.

Many Adversaries

LORD, how many adversaries I have!
How many there are who rise up against me!

Psalm 3:1, *Book of Common Prayer*

As a teenager taking a world history class from a man who was a born teacher, I was fascinated by the French Revolution and World War II. Now I barely remember the difference between Robespierre and Rommel. I've also taken a marked dislike for war, perhaps because of the lingering effects of the Vietnam War on my psyche and on that of my nation. Sometimes battle imagery does fit as a metaphor for cancer, even if I don't care for the terms used.

I had almost recovered from the shock to my system that involved major surgery, insertion of a port, four months of chemotherapy, and removal of a port. I decided this strange ovarian cancer was some sort of blip in my lifetime of relatively good health. Now that it was gone, I was going to be back to normal—the new normal, punctuated by three-month checkups.

When they found bladder cancer at the six-month CT scan, my wishful thinking quickly disappeared. I felt as if my entire body was a cancerous mass, bent on destroying me. My system was clearly toxic beyond my imagination, full of many adversaries. Two kinds of cancer cells had risen up against me! I knew that because of the ovarian cancer, I was automatically more susceptible to breast cancer. (Since then, I've discovered there's also a link between ovarian and colon cancer, and that Ashkenazi Jewish woman are more prone to get breast and ovarian cancer. I am one-fourth Ashkenazi Jew.) Clearly, the only thing to do was to put my affairs in order and prepare to die. This conclusion turned out to be wrong, for the time being.

For some women I know, the issue isn't multiple cancers but recurrence of cancer, necessitating new drug protocols. My bladder cancer, which one oncologist called a "nuisance" cancer, has returned multiple times, but hasn't required chemo. Oddly enough, the drugs I was given for ovarian cancer were also the most potent for my bladder cancer, so I was—unbeknownst to me or my gynecologic oncologist—being treated for both at the same time.

The blessing in all this—I've learned there is always a blessing—is that I am not alone in the struggle. Not only do I have amazing friends to support me, but I also have a cadre of medical professionals who are scary-smart, funny, and kind. I know that they will be with me throughout this siege, however protracted. More than a decade after the end of chemotherapy for ovarian cancer, in the context of a discussion about releasing me from his care in a year or two if all continues to go well, my doctor reassures me I will always be his patient.

Cancer is a formidable foe, but I am not helpless. God has sent me the best caregivers who will walk with me into whatever fray I must go.

Choosing Joy

You show me the path of life.
In your presence there is fullness of joy;
in your right hand are pleasures forevermore.

Psalm 16:11

The women who preceded me in this cancer experience have tried to teach me that joy is a choice. Regardless of our circumstances, we can choose to be joyful. Happiness may be dependent on positive events—I'm always happy after a clear checkup. Joy, however, is cultivated as carefully as a garden. And like a garden, it takes work.

Several annoying things occurred yesterday (none of them life-threatening), and I was full of unhappiness, forgetting to choose joy. This morning, I am trying to write my way back and pay attention to the current of joy in the river of my life. Outside, it is not yet light, but I can hear a bird chirping anyway. Maybe that's my symbol—a bird who knows that the light is coming and sings appreciatively before the fact.

In the Episcopal tradition, we sometimes speak of the dead as being "in the nearer presence of God." For me, those words are a reminder that we are already, here on Earth, in the presence of God. How could it be otherwise, when God is everywhere and in everything? (I know: the idea of *nearer* in relation to the presence of God is not logical.)

The psalm says that in God's presence (which we're already in) there is fullness of joy. Fullness of joy can be part of my experience, whether I'm headed for surgery, for chemo or radiation, or for another little "procedure."

Joy is a choice, sometimes a deliberate effort. I can mope around, as I did yesterday because I cannot control the world, or I can listen for the sound of birdsong and other evidences of God's sustaining love.

Tasting and Seeing

O taste and see that the LORD is good;
happy are those who take refuge in him.

Psalm 34:8

Having cancer offers the opportunity to learn a great deal more about my body than I ever wanted to know. Because I am being carefully monitored, I know now that I also (probably) have celiac disease, which means that I can't digest gluten. Gluten is the protein in wheat, rye, and barley that makes bread taste good; it is also added to a host of other products, such as tomato soup. I wouldn't care, except that the information about gluten intolerance threatens me with intestinal cancer if I keep ingesting gluten. I don't need another cancer. In a congregation of more than a hundred people, two of us have been diagnosed with celiac disease. So, our priest ordered special gluten-free wafers for us that she sets on the side of the paten.

Our hymn during Eucharist recently was "Taste and See," a melodious setting of Psalm 34. As I knelt to receive my special rice communion wafer and sip of wine, everything collided in my head: the song; the taste of a gluten-free body of Christ; the generous gulp of wine the chalice bearer served me, so that it nearly ran down my chin. It was only five days after another surgery, and I was not eating much or with joy.

Last Wednesday I had my fifth outpatient surgery in twenty-seven months. Strangely, in between I forget how these invasive procedures affect my body. I rarely lose my appetite; this time, however, food didn't appeal. The experience of not eating for a few days had caused me to think about fasting, about Jesus, Moses, and Elijah going without food for forty days. About how much easier fasting is when the mind is preoccupied, whether with prayer or pain.

Years ago, someone pointed out in a sermon that the exhortation of this verse seems backwards—normally, we look at food before we taste it. No, says the psalmist—eat, and you will see that the Lord is good. The whole of Christianity—or of any religious faith—is trust. Eat this thing, this cancer that is trying to eat you first, and see that the Lord is good.

Make no mistake—I don't like having cancer, and I'm not one of those people who say they wouldn't trade what they've learned from the experience. Call me shallow—I'd like my complete health back, freedom from worry about the next recurrence/checkup/surgery, and a refund of all the money I've paid out to be well. I love the people I've met. I've even adjusted a bit to being lavishly cared for and knowing I'm loved. But I'd happily go back to a life that didn't include such deep knowledge of my own mortality and that of those who are important to me.

I am still tasting and seeing. Gluten-free rice wafers are crunchier and tastier than the standard wafer. I think they'd be great with cheese. I don't like having celiac any more than I like having cancer, but I can taste and see that the Lord is good.

A New Song

He put a new song in my mouth,
a song of praise to our God.
Many will see and fear,
and put their trust in the LORD.

Psalm 40:3

This is one of the six times throughout the psalms that the writer refers to a new song, all of which are to be praise. But I want to protest; I liked the old song, thank you very much. I had worked hard—more than half a century—to get the song of my life exactly the way I wanted it. It included faith and flowers and friends, good health, good food, and enough work.

Having cancer makes me feel a similar disorientation to that I experienced when I auditioned to be in a choir. I thought we were going to perform Gabriel Faure's *Requiem*, only to discover that we were doing Frances Poulenc's *Gloria*. Some days, however, cancer feels like moving from *Gloria* to *Requiem*. I don't like this new song.

The new song sometimes requires singing jangling, discordant notes in a minor key. I experience a dramatic pause for about a month before my regular blood marker tests. A crazy movie-track theme begins to run in my head—"What if it's back? What if it's back?"

The great thing about singing in a choir is that mine is not the only voice. When I'm feeling as though only a dirge will do, someone else is doing a riff on *alleluia*. A good choir requires many voices, well-trained and not, and a director to guide them.

I'm a weak alto who needs to stand next to a strong alto to get the notes right. Otherwise, I might wander into second soprano or tenor, or an arrangement of a Christmas carol I sang in high school. Or a note that's nowhere on the page. As a newbie cancer patient, I relied on women I met who'd been through treatment before to guide me in this new song. And I had an excellent group of directors, my doctor and nurses, who had seen the music for this song before and were not sightreading the notes.

All of us—the cancer choir members and each medical professional—worked to sing a new song, even in the midst of pain and difficulty. When I was ready to begin the requiem for yet another body part, an oncologist said to me gently, "We are not there yet." Now, ten years later, we are still not there. Eventually, with the help of so many good people, I've found reasons to sing *Gloria*.

Finding Hope

But I call upon God,
*and the L*ORD *will save me.*
Evening and morning and at noon
I utter my complaint and moan,
and he will hear my voice.

Psalm 55:16-17

Some days it's easy to feel hopeless. Those days came for me most often during the last part of my chemo regimen, when I joked that I was getting a *B* as a cancer patient—bald and bloated. I may have retained my humor, but I was short on hope.

God gives us hope, and I have found that God often uses human agency to do so. I took hope from other women I met who had survived ovarian cancer five years or longer. (The statistics, which my doctor encourages his patients to ignore, offer a 50-50 chance of being alive five years after treatment.) If those women could do it, so could I. Even when I faced the reality that there were no guarantees, that the disease might recur and I might need another round of chemo later, there were women in the chemo infusion room who were showing me how to face that need gracefully and with hope.

I find hope in the children of my church. I generally see them at their dearest, not when they are ill, fretful, or throwing tantrums. They are beautiful, and they will live even if I do not. One of them has already faced chemo and made a full recovery from her childhood cancer.

Walking in the woods offers another means that God uses to give me hope. So much life goes on in such a small space! The bugs and plants and larger critters are all busily carrying out their life's purpose, indifferent to my survival, intent on their own. The algae edging toward the middle of the river, the carp swimming lazily in it, the canes growing along the water's edge are all doing exactly what they need to be doing. The trees were here before I came along, and they will outlast me. My existence does not determine the fate of the larger world. I don't find nature's indifference disheartening; much as I joke about being the center of the universe, I know that I am not.

Music and other art forms strengthen my hope. Today is the first rehearsal this year for the orchestra chorus to which I belong. Singing or listening to challenging music, visiting art museums, watching a play or a dance recital—all of these lift my heart and offer hope. Bach and Brahms, Monet and Michelangelo lived!

We take the hope that has been given wherever we find it. God has sewn hope into the very fabric of the world. Our task as we face cancer is to spend a bit of each day focusing on the hope we have appropriated as our own—then sharing that hope with others who need it, too.

Mired

Save me from the mire; do not let me sink;
let me be rescued from those who hate me
and out of the deep waters.

Psalm 69:16, *Book of Common Prayer*

As soon as I finished chemotherapy, my calendar miraculously cleared. No longer would I write *hospital* on three of every four Fridays, with doctor appointments and blood draws in between. During the first six months of 2007, I could truthfully say to most invitations, "I'm booked." Sometimes I'd offer a true friend the option of going along on a blood draw and then having lunch out, to take away the (literal) sting.

It's easy to get mired in the minutia of cancer, the ten thousand details that occupy our minds. Those of us who work during treatment have a second set of details to deal with. As our treatments continue and our strength wanes, we can feel ourselves sinking into our own version of the daily grind. It's no surprise that a synonym for mire is bog, or that we complain we are bogged down with the many appointments and tests that are part of treatment.

Despite our fatigue and need to care for basic chores, though, it's also important to do things that lift our spirits. One of my fondest memories after my major surgery is of a friend who one sunny January afternoon took me to a deli to choose my lunch (her treat) and then drove us to a local park for a picnic-in-the-car. She drove from her home an hour each way to perform that kindness, and we still both talk of it. To be out in nature, to sing, to play with babies, to visit an art gallery or museum or attend a concert—all of these are ropes to assist God in the task of rescuing us from the mire.

With everything else we have to track during treatment—some of us without family nearby to help—it's easy to think of this as one more item on the eternal to-do list. Because feeding the spirit doesn't feel as crucial as feeding the body, because we are already so tired, we are tempted to skip it. We move caring for our spirits to the list for tomorrow or next week, where it may be bumped again.

Spirit and body are related, though. Not paying attention to the needs of our spirit can be harmful to the body. Being at peace, being mindful of what feeds our inner contentment and then pursuing those activities can assist us in ways we do not know.

When I was dithering about my future during seminary, a friend who had tired of hearing me whine gave me a word picture that has stuck with me. She took part in contra dances, which are similar to folk dances. Partners changed during the movements of the dance, as they do in square dancing. She said it was a grand thing to be caught by the firm grasp of the hand of her next partner. It had *weight,* she explained. "Give the Creator some weight," she advised me. As we pray not to sink in the mire, we need to give God something to work with in bringing about our healing, in whatever way best feeds our spirit.

Given Life Again

Will you not give us life again,
that your people may rejoice in you?

Psalm 85:6

During the meeting with my gynecologic oncologist to discuss the recommended chemotherapy regimen, he told me, "This isn't your whole life. It's just going to feel that way." I also remember the session with him in which I said that the chemo regimen was beginning to feel routine. This pleased him; apparently, it was a point he wanted all his patients to arrive at, some integration of treatment with one's life.

He was also happy, however, about three-and-a-half years after I'd finished treatment when I said, "I feel as if I'm getting my life back."

"That's where we've all wanted to be, you especially," he told me.

For me, getting my life back meant I wasn't afraid to look ahead further than the next doctor's appointment. I could begin to make plans, with just a whisper—rather than a roar— in my head of "What if the cancer comes back?" I felt well; I took on some long-range commitments. When asked to teach at church (we plan the year in advance) I no longer responded, "But what if I'm in treatment?" I took on a part-time job.

The psalmist says the point of getting life again is to rejoice in God. I didn't exactly act the part of an ingrate before my cancer, and I don't walk around all day shouting hosannas now. For me, rejoicing is made up of noticing the little stuff—I just looked up from the computer in time to see a cardinal swoop by, a bright spot on a gray day. I consciously thank God at each meal, not in the perfunctory way I had before, but for each component on my plate, and the growers and producers. (This is especially easy to do once the farmers' market opens—I've been buying fresh produce from some of the growers for years.)

After cancer, some people are eager to get back to their old life, old ways of doing things. I'm not here to fault anyone's coping mechanisms, but I wonder if that's the most effective way to spend our renewed lifespans. I jettisoned some activities that had become burdensome, and facilitated the revival of my writing group, which had died of apathy. Hosting the group in my home has been a source of great joy. (It also helps me clean once in a while!)

Each of us must find our own way after treatment. But for all of us, rejoicing in God, in whatever form that takes, must become a regular part of our maintenance.

Recompense

Make us glad by as many days as you have afflicted us,
and as many years as we have seen evil.

Psalm 90:15

This Scripture seems to me the ancient equivalent of the modern cry, "I want a do-over!" For each day of affliction, I get a day of gladness; for each year of evil, I receive a year of good. Although it's appealing in some ways, many things are wrong with the idea in this verse. For starters, God doesn't afflict us. God's will for us, as my priest prays at our Wednesday morning healing Eucharist, is wholeness and healing. Secondly, the idea of an even trade is impossible. It's rare that a day is so completely full of affliction that there's no gladness to be found, a year so full of evil that we can't find any good. Life is more complicated than that.

That said, however, there is a sense of being owed something in recompense for having cancer or enduring treatment. Sometimes, getting another day to live doesn't feel like enough. We want reparations.

We forget sometimes that other people also have severe losses, illnesses, and griefs. I was always surprised when I spoke to groups of people at the applause I received, just for still being alive after surgery and chemo. What about the person who has lived with diabetes and successfully managed it for decades? The person who got a bypass surgery just in time? The parents who care for a child with muscular dystrophy? Where is the applause for them?

We need to let go of the desire for recompense, focus instead on finding those moments of joy in the midst of difficulty: a child's smile, a flower, a kind nurse, or the knowledge that we are never alone in our struggles for healing. We have not only wonderful medical professionals on our side but also, as St. Paul indicated, the Holy Spirit, who prays for us in words too deep to be spoken (Romans 8:26). Small wonder that only a few verses later Paul breaks into one of the great hymns of Scripture—*Who shall separate us from the love of Christ?* Nothing, he concludes, not even death. Not even cancer.

Looking for the Face of God

LORD, hear my prayer,
and let my cry come before you;
hide not your face from me
in the day of my trouble.

Psalm 102:1, *Book of Common Prayer*

I grew up singing hymns, many of them great tunes coupled with dreadful lyrics. There were also some exceptionally lovely hymns, with a theology and melody I can still appreciate. This verse from Psalms brings one of them to mind; Edward Mote wrote the words to "The Solid Rock." One verse begins, "When darkness veils his lovely face, I rest on his unchanging grace." I cling to this idea—God does not turn away or hide the divine face from us, but darkness can obscure it. (Somehow, I never have a problem thinking God has hidden from me when everything is going well.)

Like most of the country, we've had odd weather here in my village this summer. I've seen the most amazing cloud formations presaging a storm, dark mounds with sunlight—glorious and bright—just behind them. The sun didn't go anywhere; it was simply obscured, a visual metaphor.

Many things can veil the face of God for us: sheer pain, weariness, fear, lack of nourishment (because sometimes during treatment nothing appeals or tastes good), and boredom because of enforced rest all come quickly to mind. Perhaps the sympathy and understanding expected from friends and family—whom we count on to be the hands and feet of God—aren't there, or wear out when our disease refuses to remain in remission and continues over years instead of months.

Then it's tempting to believe God has turned away from us, that there's some heavenly hide-and-seek game going on. But God doesn't play games. God is utterly and completely *for* us, always not only *by* our side, but also *on* our side.

Here's the only thing I know—there's something big going on. I'm just a small part in it, no more important than the cardinal that just landed on the tree outside my window, but no less dear to God the Unhidden One, either.

The Other Hardest Part

Return, O my soul, to your rest,
for the LORD has dealt bountifully with you.

Psalm 116:7

I've been reading an article on fish farming in Tanzania in the latest magazine from Heifer International. One fish farmer decided to take seriously his pledge to pass on the gift of fish fingerlings he received when those fish reproduced; he taught his blind neighbor to be a fish farmer as well. The blind man recounted that the hardest part was breaking the sunbaked soil to dig a pond. Then he went on to say the other hardest part was hauling the manure without modern tools.

It made me smile, this charming sentence that's not grammatically correct in English, where *hardest* is the superlative degree, and two superlatives are not possible. Then I realized that I could use that form, however incorrect, to talk about cancer.

Because for me, *everything* was the other hardest part. The pain that stopped my life, the waiting for surgery, the diagnosis, the port, weeks of chemotherapy, loss of my hair, discovery of a second cancer, repeated surgeries for that cancer, waiting between appointments to see if the cancers had returned—all of these are the hardest part. For someone as stubborn and independent as I am, even allowing people to help me was the hardest part.

With the ovarian cancer (the dangerous one) in remission for many years, it should be getting easier to be hopeful. In some ways it is, but the fear and dread of recurrence never leave entirely. Having seen too many women back for second, third, fourth, fifth rounds of treatment I can't be complacent or say, "I've beaten it." My gynecologic oncologist says that ovarian cancer is like a dandelion head after it's past blossom, and that

87

little cancer seeds spread throughout the abdomen like dandelion seeds on the breeze. He's a thorough man, and he thoroughly washed out my abdominal cavity after the surgery. Still.

It's Holy Week, when I am supposed to be focusing on the final week of Jesus' earthly life. I think every bit of that week must have been the other hardest part. It didn't take his knowledge as the Son of God to see what was going to happen. When Jesus proposed going to Bethany, a few miles outside Jerusalem, to heal Lazarus, "doubting" Thomas said, "Let us also go, that we may die with him" (John 11:16).

Jesus never promised us an easy road or a life without burdens. He offered his followers a yoke, the kind they use on oxen. The difference is that this yoke is easy, because he's the one we're yoked with, and he carries the heaviest burdens so that I don't have to. When the burden of the other hardest part becomes too heavy, I know I've tried to shoulder part of the burden that isn't mine to carry. And I can set it down.

Songs of Gratitude

Rainspeak

forget your chores
the dishes
laundry
dusting will wait
instead
watch the droplets
insistent, coming
from a gray sky

look at the green
all but shouting
see the asparagus fern
palest of all greens
tremble

notice the drops
landing on leaves
slight pressure downward
the way the drops look
on mulberries
the squirrels
haven't eaten yet

pick up a book
settle into your chair
listen to rooftop patter

slow your busy heart
give thanks

Bright Darkness

*You, O L*ord*, are my lamp;*
my God, you make my darkness bright.

Psalm 18:29, *Book of Common Prayer*

This morning I experienced what I call a revelation of the obvious while reading this verse. It doesn't say, "you destroy my darkness" or "you obliterate my darkness." This isn't about energy-saving ceiling lights that enlighten the entire room. We aren't reading about a brightly lit stage, but a lamp, which provides light in a limited space.

It says God, a lamp, makes the darkness bright, but does not dispel the darkness, which is what I most often hope for. And yet, one of the (admittedly few) things I like about winter is early and long darkness, with lamps lit around the house, making it cozy. Yes, the darkness can get depressing, but summer's relentless brightness gets wearing as well.

Life sometimes seems to be compounded of nothing but darkness, especially when we are in treatment or headed for another surgery. But in the same way that a night light can chase away a child's fears of the dark, so the lamp that God provides can chase off the gloom of cancer's darkness.

Will the cancer go away? Maybe, for a time. But it can also come back, albeit not as regularly as evening follows day. Every evening, though, we still have lamps to light; God provides lamps for us with each cancer episode.

The psalmist likely had small, clay oil lamps that gave out little light and less heat. When I visit a lighting store, I can find many varieties of table lamps, hanging lamps, floor lamps—rows and rows of light-givers. In the same way, God has many models of lamps to send us for our cancer-darkness moments.

Friends bring food, flowers, company. Medical professionals bring their skill and compassion. Places of worship provide prayer shawls, space to offer devout prayers and praise, along with encouraging friends.

During the worst days of treatment, I lived twelve miles from my church. It could be a real effort to dress and drive there; I did so in part because of the example of another woman, some years earlier, who faithfully appeared each week during her treatment, getting weaker and more ill, but still there, a witness to God's grace. The other part, of course, was my stubbornness. I was not going to allow cancer to deprive me of my worship community.

When I walked into the church, I felt my entire body relax and allowed myself to feel the weariness I'd pushed aside. When I mentioned this to a friend, he said it was probably because I felt safe there, and that was true. Practically speaking, there were several nurses in the congregation; if anything terrible happened, they would know what to do. Beyond that, the brightness of people who cared for me kept the darkness away.

Through the Eyes of Love

For your steadfast love is before my eyes...

Psalm 26:3, *Book of Common Prayer*

I remember waking in the recovery room, scared to reach under the thin blanket to see if I had an incision in my abdomen. If the mass was cancer, during surgery to remove it, my doctor would have put in a port for intraperitoneal chemo. I could not check; I was too afraid.

As I gained consciousness, I was aware of my doctor, a tall, dark-haired man, standing to the left of the bed. He spoke four words: "Good news, no cancer." Surely that was God's love before my eyes! I would not have to endure the indignities of cancer treatment. I could recover from surgery and go home, live my life. Even after he asked permission to send slides of my cells to a specialist at Harvard, I had a 90 percent chance of being cancer-free, because, as he told me, "Our guys in pathology are good. Ninety percent of the time, Harvard agrees with them."

Over the next few weeks, instances that were obvious signs of God's love were visible:

- the friend who sat all night in a recliner the night after my surgery, alert to my smallest movement
- others who visited, sent or brought gifts or food after I returned home, as well as those who helped me run errands or walk in the woods
- the amazing nurses and personal assistants who made a week in the hospital bearable, and the nurses who later made chemo bearable as well
- friends who read to me, in the hospital and after I went home

- the editor at my freelance job, who told me not to worry, the project was still mine
- my priest, who brought communion to the house, despite her cat allergies

At my checkup three weeks after surgery, my gynecologic oncologist sat down and said, "It's as we feared—it's cancer." He shocked me; I hadn't expected the Harvard doctor to whom my slides had been sent to contradict the postsurgery announcement. The friend who had driven me to the appointment had offered to join me in the examining room, but I'd refused, certain of my escape. It was only me and my notebook of questions, most of which, as my doctor said, had become largely irrelevant.

The time he took with me that day, and all the other days, was God's love before my eyes, disguised in a long white lab coat. "It's all good," another survivor says. Some days, frankly, I have trouble with that idea. But I'm learning to see that it's all God's love, right there before my eyes, if only I will look.

At All Times

I will bless the LORD at all times;
his praise shall continually be in my mouth.

Psalm 34:1

The verse doesn't say, I will bless the Lord except on days when my country is at war, or days when my family is in jeopardy, or days when I must face a CT scan or a chemotherapy treatment.

A chemo day is not an obvious choice for having the praise of God in my mouth. Receiving chemo can be boring, moderately uncomfortable, and filled with side effects that after a while begin to remind me of the plagues of Egypt. And yet reasons remained for blessing God during my four months of chemo.

Chemo days were different from the rest of my life. They provided time off from being responsible, days when I knew I couldn't control anything. Because of the strong anti-nausea medications, I wasn't permitted to drive; someone had to take me to the hospital. It wasn't my job to make sure the car was clean or had gas, to navigate snowy roads or 5 p.m. traffic on the drive back home.

Once at the hospital, I could do nothing. Someone else was in charge of making sure I got the right meds, finding the best vein to insert the IV, and accessing my port. A pick-ax headache from the meds wasn't solely my problem, but a concern for my chemo nurse to chart and to remedy. I didn't even head to the bathroom alone—couldn't, in fact, because of all the cords and IV bags; if I wanted to walk the few feet from my recliner to the bathroom, a nurse accompanied me and my IV pole. My only task was to keep from going stark mad in my recliner, aimlessly rotating amusement among crossword puzzles, light reading, quilting, and snacking.

Some women allowed the Benadryl "megadoze" to do its work and passed the day in a pleasant fog. I was too frightened, especially at first, to allow my body to do that. Other women watched television, but I don't much care for the medium. One brought a CD player, but doing so felt like one more thing for me to take care of. Being the only conscious patient gave me the unanticipated pleasure of talking with Vikki, my chemo nurse, to the extent that her duties allowed it.

After the chemo finished dripping, someone arrived to drive me home. Occasionally we stopped at a restaurant for a light supper; at other times, friends provided a meal. No one expected anything of me. I didn't have to come home and get to work; in fact, my employers preferred that I not work. (After I sent in one manuscript that I had carefully crafted, my editor joked to her boss, "They're giving Judy really good drugs.") My only task was to call Charlotte, my priest, who asked me to report in. Despite baldness, bloating, neuropathy, ringing in my ears, and a headache, chemo days were oddly restful days, days to bless the Lord.

Remission Bridge

For you have rescued me from every trouble,
and my eye has seen the ruin of my foes.

Psalm 54:7, *Book of Common Prayer*

This week was my regular four-month checkup for one of my cancers. Only two "miniscule" spots showed up, and my oncologist thought it proper to ignore them for now. I am thinking of myself as being rescued, my cancer-cell foes in ruin. I still consider myself to be in remission. This morning, I suddenly visualized the word *remission* as a steel bridge, one of the fancy nineteenth-century bridges that worked curlicues into the design: humps of the *m* and *n*, curves of the *s*'s, a rounded *o*.

To drive from the southern tip of the Florida peninsula to Key West, as I did several times while teaching in West Palm Beach after college, one drives on a two-lane highway that includes the Seven-Mile Bridge. It's easy to panic on that bridge, especially driving a van full of high school students traveling to visit Ernest Hemingway's home. The water stretches on both sides; in the mid-1970s, there were stretches of it without guardrails and no room to pull over. (It's since been improved.) But it did get us where we were going.

To me and to my friends with cancer, *remission* is a blessed word. It's not the final destination, though. It's a way to live between here and there, whether *there* is another recurrence, complete healing, or death. It's a span over the water of our lives with cancer—because the cancer is there, in the same way that water under a bridge is there.
Cancer is the fact we live with, even when we choose to ignore it.

In Morning and Evening Prayer Rite I, the formula that the priest uses to pronounce forgiveness after we confess our sins includes the words "grant you absolution and remission of all your sins." We don't do much remitting any more. It's a term from Latin; it means "to send back," and that's a great thing to do with money (the original context) or sin. The third meaning in my Merriam-Webster is the definition I love—relax.

When we are in remission, we relax a bit, enjoy the scenery, blessedly free from chemo, surgery, radiation, blood work, scans, and scopes. We take deep breaths, feel again what "normal" might be like, even if what we have is a "new normal." We allow the sturdy remission bridge to support us over the choppy, white-capped water, and we smile in the sunlight.

Rising Waters

Save me, O God, for the waters have risen up to my neck.

Psalm 69:1, *Book of Common Prayer*

That verse came to mind last week as I readied for one of those dreaded "little procedures." I was unfamiliar with this one, and I'd not had time to begin reading the explanatory literature before my name was called. I was given a blue paper gown and told to change into it. When I came back out, clutching the back of the gown, the nurse was putting waterproof pads on the examining table.

"They irrigate as they examine the bladder, so I'm putting all these pads down," she explained. "You've had one of these before, haven't you?"

"Nope—I had no idea."

I've learned that despite my independence, it's a good idea to have someone with me when I'm seeing a specialist. Maggie accompanied me that Tuesday, bringing her earthy and hearty humor. Standing at my head, she declared, "Let's sing water songs! Come on. 'Row, row, row your boat.'" We moved on to "Michael Row the Boat Ashore," and "Got Any Rivers You Think Are Uncrossable?" Maggie objected, though, to my suggestion of "On Jordan's Stormy Banks."

"No storms!" she begged, but I sang it anyway. Although I wasn't standing at the Jordan—a metaphor for death—I was casting a wistful eye, if not "to Canaan's fair and happy land," then at least to the land of no tumors.

It was not to be. During the procedure, I could clearly observe the growths and was unsurprised when the oncologist recommended surgery. As I was mopping up and changing back into my civilian clothes, I heard laughter coming from the examining room. The two women were laughing, but I was feeling decidedly Job-like as I pulled on my jeans and sweater. The passages that came to mind weren't Job's "Though he slay me, yet will I trust him," or even "I know that my redeemer liveth" (Job 13:15; 19:25 KJV). No, I was thinking of that lesser-known verse, "Will you not look away from me for a while, let me alone until I swallow my spittle?" (Job 7:19 KJV).

When I came out of the dressing room, Maggie and the nurse, a no-nonsense woman who was about my age, explained the joke to me. The nurse's stance when her washer, dryer, and hot water heater all failed in two days' time was to eye her refrigerator and dishwasher and to challenge them, "Bring it on!"

Her first words to me, however, were, "Now don't you go feeling sorry for yourself." As we walked down the hall, she reminded me that God cares for the sparrows and for us.

I surmise that she sees many people who, quite reasonably to my mind, succumb to self-pity. That door was closed for me. I was left instead with the joys of friendship, laughter, and song.

Remembering Who We Are

I will call to mind the deeds of the LORD;
I will remember your wonders of old.

Last week in her sermon, my priest mentioned that over and over in the Hebrew Bible the people are reminded of their history. Why would anyone want to remember a time of being enslaved? Remembering their distress, as well as their triumphs, however, was designed to remind the people of Israel who they were and how God had delivered them.

After treatment or surgery, cancer patients sometimes want to forget everything about their experience. "Put it all back the way it was!" we may cry, not wanting to know how impossible that is. Yet probably you know, as I do, people who return to smoking after successful treatment, people who never find a support group because they don't "need" one. And maybe they don't—how can I know or prescribe what's best for everyone?

As a member of Survivors Teaching Students, I am privileged to join a few other women in my area to remember and share my story. Some of the survivors who've been invited to join us have not been able to do so. "It brings it all back," one said, after listening to one of our sessions. Yes, it does. While we don't dwell on the wretchedness of hair loss, nausea, or fatigue, these realities do come up. Our audience is comprised of future doctors—almost always young people in good health—and we don't want to minimize the trauma or suffering of cancer treatment.

We bring it all back to remind ourselves of who we are. We are survivors, an overused word. The support group I'm part of refers to us instead as thrivers, going beyond mere dreary survival. Whatever term we choose, whether we can admit it, we are people whose lives will never be the same, affected not only by the disease but also by all the people we meet in Cancerland—doctors, nurses, and other patients all have something to share.

The support group for women cancer survivors that I joined is organized into smaller groups. Mine met for lunch at a chain restaurant recently. At the end of the meal, each of us shared where we were now in our cancer experience, rejoicing with all those still healthy, committing to pray (or visualize or send energy or whatever it is we do) for the women who are facing increasing numbers. The woman next to me leaned over at one point and said quietly, "The women at the next table are getting an earful!" It was true—names of cancer drugs and tumor marker numbers rolled easily off our tongues, and we spoke loudly to be heard over the restaurant's din.

We laugh and we hug, glad for a reason to be glad for the people we've met because of cancer, if not for the disease itself. We remind ourselves of who we are and where we've been and are strengthened in that remembering.

Revived to Rejoice

Will you not revive us again,
so that your people may rejoice in you?

Psalm 85:6

I belong to a local women's support group for cancer survivors, which admits new members twice annually. My cohort was the tenth such group, limited to fifteen women who would be cared for during an intense ten weeks together. We met each Thursday for a session of qigong (similar to tai chi), dinner, and focused conversation. One evening during our group sharing time, the facilitator asked in her sweet Southern voice, "What keeps you going?"

Nearly every woman prefaced her answer by saying, "That's a tough question." That evening in group we went around the semicircle and gave our off-the-cuff answers. Most women related their need to survive for family members: aging parents, beloved children and grandchildren. My parents are gone; my brother and his wife live nearly two hundred miles away, and we see each other infrequently. I am single and childless. "I have a book to write," I said.

Her query reminded me of the scene in the film *Princess Bride,* when Miracle Max asks the "mostly-dead" Westley, "What do you have that's worth living for?" Each of us gave our version of Westley's response to Miracle Max: "True love."

Chemo had made me feel mostly dead. I seemed to sleep more hours than I was awake; when I was awake, I wasn't always interested in food—except for mashed potatoes and mac and cheese—and I wasn't thinking well. One beautiful spring day, near the end of chemo, I was ready to let go and finish dying.

I needed to be revived again, just as the Israelites of this psalm needed to be.

For the psalmist, the reason to be revived was to rejoice in God. That's a bit abstract for me. Possibly the writer meant some sort of ritual rejoicing; many of the Hebrew religious holidays centered on joyous feasts.

Today we celebrated Epiphany, the church feast that commemorates the arrival of the magi, and the light that has risen for the Gentiles. I was able to rejoice in one of the chalice bearers, a college student I'd sponsored for confirmation several years before; she looked all grown up now! After church, the current crop of teenage girls surrounded me, recounting their first adventures with downhill skiing. I then had lunch with one of them, my present confirmand. As always after such a day, I marvel and rejoice in the dear young people around me.

The need to choose joy every day, every moment, is one of the cancer support group's emphases. I now wear a bracelet that one of the members made, with a heart-shaped charm that says *Joy* on it. No matter our circumstances, even in chemo, we can choose to rejoice in God, in all of the gifts God sends daily, to revel in being alive, in true love all around us.

The Promise of Presence

He shall call upon me and I will answer him;
I am with him in trouble;
I will rescue him and bring him to honor.

Psalm 91:15, *Book of Common Prayer*

The Bible is filled with extravagant promises. As my faith has aged along with my body, I've learned not to take these assurances as literal guarantees. Promises of long life, of healing, of moving mountains—all these I regard as simply whistling in the dark, the writer hoping against hope that they are true, the way that verifiable statements such as "the sun rises in the east" are true.

I'm not sure it matters whether or not they are literally true, and for every instance in which they appear to be, I can find two examples of where they clearly are not. Yet, faithful to my earliest training, I find it difficult not to "cling to the promises," as we used to sing.

Psalm 91 is one of my (many) favorite psalms. This morning I found it easy to ignore the promise in verse 3 of being delivered from the deadly pestilence, when I know that one version of pestilence has been growing in my bladder's lumen—a *not* illuminating thought. When I reached verse 15, however, I was ensnared by the promise of presence.

What I want—and what I think most people want—is the sense that we are not alone as we struggle with our disease and its ramifications. Those of us without spouses—or with partners so hurt and sad and scared by our illness that they have no comfort left to offer us—may feel especially vulnerable. How much can and should we burden our friends or our children? Who will accompany us to surgery, to treatment?

Those are questions with which we may need to wrestle. Still, we can rest in the reality that God does not abandon us in trouble; God is an all-weather, all-terrain friend. Walking through the valley of the shadow of death is frightening, but it's not a solo journey. We are not asked to be Amelia Earhart or one of the other early pilots flying alone through the night, unsure if we will survive the journey. We have company.

Some people can sense the presence of God or angels; one of my friends hears an audible voice. I don't. Nevertheless, I am aware of God being present in the actions of my friends, who begin offering help almost before I need it. Grace goes ahead of us, getting things ready. Though we may be solitary, we are not alone. We are accompanied by one who has walked a road of anguish in a human body, one who knew fear and the hardship of a prayer that didn't receive the hoped-for answer. We are not alone.

Being Freed

I called to the LORD in my distress;
the LORD answered by setting me free.

Psalm 118:5, *Book of Common Prayer*

At first, these lines strike me as an example of mismatched ideas. For a prayer and its consequence, I might pair distress with relief, or bondage with freedom, but not distress with freedom as a response. The more I've thought about it, though, it seems the psalmist may have been right.

In our adult education sessions at church recently, we've been looking at metaphors and parables. Jesus is the True Vine, and we are the branches, but the truth is that the branches can put forth all sorts of shoots that need to be lopped off, because they detract from the main purpose of fruit-bearing. In the same way, our lives can easily become luxuriant with lots of interesting vines that are unproductive. It's not always possible to tell whether a new endeavor will bear fruit, or even if our results will be the desired fruit. Sometimes I've thought I was producing grapes and ended up with olives instead.

I am not a person who is always positive, grateful for my cancer. This does not mean, however, that I am blind to the gifts—there doesn't seem to be a better word—this disease has brought me. Because in my distress, I was set free from some things that were never going to bear fruit.

Some people I know manage to maintain most of their lives during cancer treatment. I'm full of admiration for the women I've met who keep their jobs and their households, even if they lose their hair. I did keep my job, but as a freelancer, I could stop for a nap whenever I needed one. As a single woman, I could let dishes or laundry go. In general, though, I think people expect less of someone undergoing chemo or radiation. Treatment gives us permission to let go of some of the burden we may not have been aware we were carrying.

A cancer diagnosis also pulls us up short, reminding us of the reality we may have been ignoring in our busy lives—we, too, are mortal. In light of that fact, how do we wish to spend whatever time we have remaining? What activities that we've had to curtail because of treatment do we most miss? What new practices will we add? Several women I know have added cancer advocacy to their calendars, fitting in walks, programs, and meetings. Some of us added a bit of therapy for our mental health. Some made or revised "bucket lists" to complete.

Many people want everything to go back to the way it was before their diagnosis. I understand that and I cannot judge it; I simply can't go there. For me, the questions had to include, What will I let go? What unproductive shoots will I prune to make room for new growth? How can I be free of some of the tasks that were once a joy but have become a burden? Cancer has given me the opportunity to examine my life and be set free.

What Do You Need?

[The LORD] gives justice to those who are oppressed,
and food to those who hunger.
The LORD sets the prisoners free;
the LORD opens the eyes of the blind;
the LORD lifts up those who are bowed down;
the LORD loves the righteous;
the LORD cares for the stranger;
he sustains the orphan and widow....

Psalm 146:6–8, *Book of Common Prayer*

When I read those verses this morning, I thought about the comprehensiveness of the Lord's provision. God is in every case the actor; we are the recipients of God's grace. Regardless of the need—justice, food, freedom, sight, raising, love, care, sustenance—God is able to meet that need.

Need isn't the same as want. I am prone to recurrent cases of "the wants." Sometimes I make lists of them, just so I don't forget that I want a manicure or a new pair of shoes. And then a tornado rips through the Southeast, and I realize how much I have already, or a friend faces surgery and I remember my own fears before my surgery and the blessings of being healthy.

When we are in the midst of cancer treatment, our needs are concentrated. We need to tolerate the regimen, we need our tumor marker numbers to go down and our blood numbers to stay up, we need rest and nutritious food. Life becomes stripped down to its essence when we are bald and bloated and weary from the chemo. I didn't feel the need for a new outfit (though

I was happy to receive hats and prayer shawls in abundance). I needed courage and grace; I asked people to pray that I would have a sufficient supply of both.

I find—several years after chemo—that it's easy for me to forget what is important and what is just part of living in a consumerist society. Being with other cancer survivors or speaking to future doctors or nurses helps to ground me in the reality that I don't need much. I have my health right now. I can't know what the next checkup will reveal. But I have today, filled with all I need and the knowledge that God is able to provide for any needs I have.

Postlude

Writing a book and dealing with cancer both require the help and kindness of many people. My endless thanks to the many folks who kept me going during the tough times:

Friends:
The four women who waited during my first big surgery and made the right decision for me when I could not: Mary Beth Pringle, Charlotte Collins Reed, Kat Walter, and Mary Jo Werthman White
The women who provided post-op care at home—theirs and mine—after each surgery. Particular thanks to Patricia Henrich, Adrianne Oliss, and the late Elizabeth Visick. They never failed to give rides and counsel, as well as the requisite post-op poached eggs. Patricia spent the night of my big surgery in a recliner in my room, just in case I needed an advocate.
Visitors who came to the hospital and my home, particularly those who traveled far to be with me, some of them doing so more than once, and the man who called every day during treatment and made sure I wasn't alone at Christmas
Providers of cards, food, flowers, gifts, prayer shawls, and a lap quilt to take to chemo
Companions and note takers for doctor visits
Drivers to surgery, appointments, and chemotherapy sessions
Alternative medicine healers
Therapists and spiritual directors
People who prayed and offered hugs
The women of Noble Circle Project, a local cancer support group, for so many things, as well as the folks from Maple Tree Alliance, Survivors Teaching Students, and other support groups
My priest and the people of Christ Episcopal Church, Springfield, Ohio, especially the women of Peace and Patches
Special thanks to long-term friends Gary W. Barker, Lori Greenawalt, Eric Helmuth, and Alicia Moffitt for nurturing, sustaining care and support through more decades than we will admit.
Karen Herzog, who became a publicist over lunch one day

And the medical people:
Oncologists, surgeons, radiologists, anesthesiologists, phlebotomists, aides, the people who keep warm blankets for CT scans and tuck in their patients, and nurses—those angels of mercy.
Special thanks to Vikki Wagner, my chemo nurse, and to Jacqueline Roethlisberger for her excellent care and listening ear. To Dr. Thomas J. Reid—whose skill, skepticism, humor, patience, and use of metaphor made this journey easier than it might have been—my endless gratitude.

Also writer friends who have encouraged me and edited this work. These women in particular have shaped this work:

Longtime writing group member Mary Jo Werthman White (who stayed for six hours while major surgery was ongoing and was with me when I learned I had cancer) gave many of these meditations a first edit years ago. She is an example to me of persistence, with both a book of poetry and a novel in print.

Wendy Widder Huisken, with whom I've traded pages to edit since 2021, and her sister, Suzy Krebs, who came in for the final edit. Working with Wendy has been an amazing and unexpected gift. She has read many words, some not in this book, and used her theological training to make sure I said what I meant to say. Our Zoom meetings every other week with ten pages each to edit, plus her encouraging comments, kept the wheels on the bus of this book. We continue to disagree about commas and italics, but those are the only areas in which we are not in harmony. All errors are my own.

My book designer, Victoria Brzustowicz (who also designed my website) makes collaborating via Zoom calls both simple and enjoyable. I wanted to reach through the computer and hug her from a couple states away.

To list all the names of people and their kindnesses would add many pages to this work. I hope you each recognize yourself and know how much you are loved.

Bonus Pages: How to Encourage a Cancer Patient

Send cards, maybe every other week, with a Bible verse, if she (or he) is that kind of person. They do not all need to be serious; funny cards are good.

Send reading material, nothing hard or long. Poetry can be very soothing and helpful. A friend came to the hospital and read to me from Billy Collins' poetry. My favorites include the funny prose prayers of Brian Doyle, such as those in his books *The Kind of Brave You Wanted to Be, The Book of Uncommon Prayer,* and *Leaping: Revelations and Epiphanies.* Think carefully about sending cancer memoirs; they can be discouraging. Music is also healing; select music you find restful and encouraging.

Send a prayer shawl of your choosing, maybe one from your place of worship, even if it's summer. Cancer patients are often cold. Buy or make a hat, very soft. A friend knit one for me using yarn named "Oh, my" for its softness.

There's a lot of waiting around with cancer—doctors, chemo, CT scans—so you might provide some small things to do: a wordsearch or crossword puzzle book, a coloring book for adults with markers or colored pencils, or a small sketchbook. Just something little and light to pass time.

Make targeted, focused suggestions for help. "Do you need anything?" or "How can I help?" isn't as effective as "I'd like to bring you dinner one night this week. Which night would work best for you and what sounds good right now?" Offer to do some light housework—a friend did dishes for me one evening, a blessing.

Here are some gifts of help I've received or heard of others receiving:
- giving tickets to a ballet, or a concert, or to a theater performance
- raking leaves or mowing lawns
- providing meals, especially those pre-packaged in individual serving sizes

113

- driving to appointments
- sitting in on conversations with health professionals to be another set of ears and eyes
- offering to go with her to choose a wig (I'm not a fan of wigs, because they are hot and scratchy. But that's just me.)

Money is a sensitive topic, but if you are gifted with organizational skills, math prowess, or negotiation power, you might help with the bills and insurance statements that will come in a deluge from multiple sources. Most hospitals and doctors will allow payment plans; many also have income-based reductions in services, which they may not mention.

If you're bringing food, always check for preferences and food allergies. Mouth sores from chemo are common. Your best bet is always soft food—I went through an extended mac-and-cheese/mashed-potato phase. As a friend says, "Comfort food should not be interesting." Think of things that go down easily, such as sorbets and cheesecake. My intro to chemo notes from the hospital actually recommended cheesecake as a nice snack, because of the calories and the fact that it's cool and creamy.

(Your friend can take off any weight gain later; the extra pounds will likely come anyway because of the chemotherapy steroids.) In a perfect world, you'd also consider nutritional value—will this food help her body mend and grow strong? Failing that, at least let it be attractive and tasty. Go easy on spices of all kinds—I developed a sensitivity to salt, which I normally love.

Take your friend out in nature, even if she's a city gal and it's winter. One of my happiest post-surgery memories is of the sunny winter day when a friend took me to the deli, bought our lunch, and drove us to the local park, where we sat in the car all wrapped up, admiring bare sycamore branches and squirrels. We are meant to be connected to nature, and it has something to offer us in every season.

Acknowledgments

The following poems were first published in these journals.

"Scanxiety" in *Common Threads* 2022

"Controlled Burn" in *Sycamore* Fall 2016

Judy A. Johnson has spent her life working with words, as an English teacher, college reference librarian, textbook editor, and freelance writer. A published poet, her work has won local and regional awards. Her previous collection of meditations, *A Week to Pray About It*, was published in 2006, shortly before her cancer symptoms manifested. An Episcopalian with a Baptist background and a master's degree in theological studies from the Methodist Theological School in Ohio, she is active in her church's teaching ministry. She blogs at judyjohnsonwrites.weebly.com.

www.ingramcontent.com/pod-product-compliance
Lightning Source LLC
Chambersburg PA
CBHW051214120626
46547CB00013B/1344